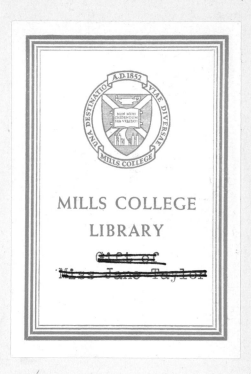

ESSAYS IN APPLICATION

ESSAYS

IN APPLICATION

ESSAYS
IN APPLICATION

BY

HENRY VAN DYKE

NEW YORK
CHARLES SCRIBNER'S SONS
1906

PREFACE

THE forces that impel action reside
in temperament. The ideals and convictions that guide it are hidden in the
mind and heart. A man moves slowly
or swiftly, he does his work weakly or
strongly, according to the energy that
is in him. But the direction of his life,
this way or that way, follows the un-
seen influence of what he admires and
loves and believes in.

It is not easy to take stock of these
controlling ideals and convictions, and
estimate them at their true value. It
is harder still to arrange and order them
in a system—clear, logical, consistent
—a philosophy of life. Few men have
the ability to make such a total state-

[v]

ment of their spiritual assets. Even for those who might be able to do it after a fashion, it is difficult to find the time, because they are actively engaged in the business of living.

But every now and then, in writing or in speaking, a man who takes his affair seriously has occasion to meet one or another of the problems of life in a way that calls him to get at his inmost convictions and to apply them to the matter in hand. It is not always possible, nor often necessary, to give an elaborate description of his point of view, or to trace the paths of inheritance or reasoning by which he has reached it. These are things that will probably betray themselves, clearly enough, in his work. Whether he be materialist or idealist, radical or conservative, optimist or pessimist or meliorist, what he has to do is just to stand where he belongs, and to put his ideals in application to the question before him.

That which is spoken or written in this way may have some value, proportionate to its lucidity and sincerity, as a partial showing of the practical conclusions to which certain principles lead. And if, as I believe, life is the test of thought, rather than thought the test of life, we should be able to get light on the real worth of a man's theories, ideals, beliefs, by looking at the shape which they would give to human existence if they were faithfully applied.

It is in this way that the chapters of this book have been written, and thus I should like to have the reader take them. I have tried to touch on certain points in education, in politics, in literature, in religion, in the conduct of life, from the standpoint of one who wishes to be guided in every-day judgments and affairs by a sane idealism. The book makes no claim to be a defense, or even a statement, of a complete system of philosophy or faith. It is simply a collection of essays in application.

CONTENTS

I

IS THE WORLD GROWING BETTER?

No man knows, of a certainty, the answer to this question.

If it were an inquiry into the condition of the world's pocket-book, or farm, or garden, or machine-house, or library, or school-room, the answer would be easy. Six million more spindles whirling in the world's workshop in 1903 than in 1900; eight hundred million more bushels of wheat in the world's grain-fields than in 1897; an average school-attendance gaining 145 per cent. between 1840 and 1888, while the population of Europe increased only 33 per cent. So the figures run in every department. No doubt the world is busier, richer, better fed, and probably it knows more, than ever before.

I am not one of those highly ethereal and supercilious people who can find nothing in this to please them, and who cry lackadaisically: " What is all this worth?" I am honest enough to confess to a sense of satisfaction when my little vegetable garden rewards my care with an enlarged crop, or when my children bring home a good report from school. Why should not a common-sense philanthropy lead us to feel in the same way about the improved condition and the better reports of the big world to which we belong? Of course our satisfaction is checked and shadowed, often very darkly shadowed, by the remembrance of those who are left behind in the march of civilization— the retarded races, the benighted classes, the poor relations, of the world. But our sympathy with them is much more likely to be helpful if it is hopeful, than if it is despairing. I do not think it necessary to cultivate melancholy or misanthropy as a preparation for beneficence.

A generous man ought to find something cheerful and encouraging to his own labours, in the knowledge that the world is growing "better off."

But is it growing better? That's another question, and a far more important one. What is happening to the world itself, the owner of all this gear, the prosperous old adventurer whose wealth, according to Mr. Gladstone, increased twice as much during the first seventy years of the nineteenth century as it had done during the eighteen hundred years preceding? Is this marvellous increase of goods beneficial to the character of the race? Or is it injurious? Or has it, perhaps, no deep or definite influence one way or the other?

You know how hard it is to come to a clear and just conclusion on such points as these, even in the case of an individual man. Peter Silvergilt's wealth has grown from nothing to three hundred million dollars during the last fifty years; but are you sure that Peter's personality is better, finer, nobler, more admirable than it was when he was a telegraph-boy earning ten dollars a week? William Wiseman has a world-wide fame as a scholar; it is commonly reported that he has forgotten more than most men ever knew; but can you trust William more implicitly to be fair and true and generous than when he was an obscure student just beginning to work for a degree in philosophy?

When we try to apply such questions,

not to a single person, but to the world at large, positive and mathematical answers are impossible. The field of inquiry is too vast. The facts of racial character are too secret and subtle.

But a provisional estimate of the general condition of the world from the point of view of goodness, comparing the present with the past—a probable guess at the direction in which the race is moving morally—this is something that we may fairly make. Indeed, if you think and care much about your brother men you can hardly help making it, and upon the colour of this guess the tone of your philosophy depends. If the colour is dark, you belong among the pessimists, who cannot be very happy, though they may sometimes be rather useful. If the colour is bright, you are what men call an optimist, though I think George Eliot's word,

[5]

"meliorist," would be a more fitting name.

For what is it, after all, that we can venture to claim for this old world of ours, at most? Certainly not that it is altogether good, nor even that it is as good as it might be and therefore ought to be. Police-stations and prisons and wars are confessions that some things are wrong and need correction. The largest claim that a cheerful man who is also a thoughtful man—a child of hope with his eyes open—dares to make for the world is that it is better than it used to be, and that it has a fair prospect of further improvement. This is meliorism, the philosophy of actual and possible betterment; not a high-stepping, trumpet-blowing, self-flattering creed, immediately available for advertising purposes; but a modest and sober faith, useful for consolation in those hours of despondency and personal disappointment when the grasshopper and the critic both become a burden, and for encouragement to more earnest effort in those hours of cheer when a high-tide of the spirit fills us with good-will to our fellow-men.

I asked John Friendly the other day: "Do you think the world is growing better?"

"Certainly," said he, with a smile like sunrise on his honest face, "I haven't the slightest doubt of it."

"But what makes you so sure of it."

"Why, it must be so! Look at all the work that is being done to-day to educate people and help them into better ways of living. All this effort must count for something. The wagon must move with so many horses pulling at it. The world can't help growing better!"

Then he left me, to go down to a meeting of his "Citizens' Committee for the Application of the Social Boycott to Political Offenders" (which frequently adjourns without a quorum). Immediately afterward I passed the door of the "Michael T. Moriarty Republi-cratic Club"—wide open and crowded. On my way up the avenue I saw a liquor-saloon on every block—and all busy. The news-stands were full of placards announcing articles in the magazines— "Graft in Chicago," "The Criminal Calendar of Millionaires," "St. Louis, the Bribers' Paradise," "The Plunder of Philadelphia." Head-lines in the yellow journals told of "Immense Slaughter in Manchuria," "Russia Ripe for Revolution." "The Black Hand Terror in the Bronx," "Gilded Gambling-Dens of the Four Hundred," "Diamonds and Divorce."

John Friendly's cheerful *a priori* confidence in the betterment of the world seemed to need reinforcement. Some of the horses are pulling his way, no doubt, but a good many appear to be pulling the other way. Under such conditions the wagon might stick fast, or go backward. Possibly it might be pulled to pieces. Who can measure, in the abstract, the comparative strength of the good and the evil forces? Who can tell beforehand which way the tug-of-war must go?

The only sound and satisfactory method is to bring out the foot-rule of fact and apply it to the tracks of the wagon. Has it moved? How fast, how far, which way?

"Growing better" is a phrase about which a company of college professors would probably have a long preliminary dispute; but plain people understand it well enough for practical purposes.

There are three factors in it. When we say that a man grows better, we mean that, in the main, he is becoming more just, and careful to do the right thing; more kind, and ready to do the helpful thing; more self-controlled, and willing to sacrifice his personal will to the general welfare. Is the world growing better in this sense? Is there more justice, more kindness, more self-restraint, among the inhabitants of earth than in the days of old?

Of course, when we consider a question like this, before even a modest guess at the answer is possible, we must be willing to take a long view and a wide view. The world, like the individual man, has its moods and its vagaries, its cold fits and its hot fits, its backslidings and its repentances, its reactions and its revivals. An advance made in one century may be partly lost in the next, and regained with interest in a later century. One nation may be degenerating, under local infections of evil, while others are improving. There may be years, or regions, of short harvest in the field of morals, just as there are in the cotton-field or the corn-field. The same general conditions that work well for the development of most men, may prove unfavourable to certain races. Civilization seems to oppress and demoralize some tribes to the point of extinction. Liberty is a tonic too strong for certain temperaments; it intoxicates them. But what we have to look at is not the local exception, nor the temporary reaction: it is the broad field as far as we can see it, the general movement as far as we can trace it. And as I try to look at the question in this way, clearly and steadily, it seems to me that the world is really growing better:

[11]

not in every eddy, but in the main current of its life; not in a straight line, but with a winding course; not in every respect, but in at least two of the three main points of goodness; not swiftly, but slowly, surely, really growing better.

Take the matter of justice. The world's sense of equity, its desire to act fairly and render to every man his due, is expressed most directly in its laws. Who can fail to see a process of improvement in the spirit and temper of legislation, a conscientious effort to make the law more efficient in the protection of human rights and more just in the punishment of offences?

In Shakespeare's time, for example, a woman's existence, in the eye of the law, was merged in that of her husband. A man could say of his wife: "She is my goods, my chattels; she is my house, my household stuff, my field. my barn, my

[12]

horse, my ox, my anything." The very presents which he gave her were still his property. He could beat her. He could deprive her of the guardianship of her children. It was not until the end of the seventeenth century that the law secured her right to the separate use of her property, and not until the middle of the nineteenth century that the legislation of Great Britain and America began to recognize and protect her as a person, entitled to work and receive wages, to dispose of her own earnings, to have an equal share with her husband in the guardianship of their children. Surely it is an immense gain in justice that woman should be treated as a human being.

This gain is most evident, of course, in those nations which are leading the march of civilization. But I think we can see traces of it elsewhere. The abolition of child-marriage and the practical extinction of the *suttee* in India, the decline of the cruelly significant fashion of "foot-binding" in China, the beginning of the education of girls in Egypt, are hints that even the heathen world is learning to believe that woman may have a claim to justice.

In the same way we must interpret the laws for the protection of the young against cruelty, oppression, and injustice. Beginning with the Factory Act of 1833 and the Mines and Collieries Act of 1842 in England, there has been a steadily increasing effort to diminish and prevent the degradation of the race by the enslavement of childhood to labor. Even the parent's right of control, says the modern world, must be held in harmony with the child's right to life and growth, mental, moral, and physical. The law itself must recognize the injustice of dealing with young delinquents as if they were old and hardened criminals. No more herding of children ten and twelve years old in the common jail! Juvenile courts and probation officers, asylums and reformatories: an intelligent and systematic effort to reclaim the young life before it has fallen into hopeless bondage to crime: this is the spirit of civilized legislation to-day. In 1903 no less than ten of the American States enacted special statutes with this end in view.

The great change for the better in modern criminal law is another proof that the world is growing more just. Brutal and degrading methods of execution, such as crucifixion, burying alive, impaling, disembowelling, breaking on the wheel: the judicial torture of prisoners and unwilling witnesses by the thumb-screw, the strappado, and the rack: cruel and agonizing penalties of various kinds have been abolished, not merely by way of concession to humanity, but with the purpose of maintaining justice in purity and dignity.

The world has been learning to discriminate more carefully between the degrees of crime. In the eighteenth century men were condemned to death for forgery; for stealing from a shop to the value of five shillings or from a house to the value of forty shillings; for malicious injury to trees, cattle, or fish-ponds; for the cutting of hop-bands from the poles in a plantation. Within eighty years capital punishment has been inflicted in England for sheep-stealing and for robbery from a house. The laws of Pennsylvania at the time of the Revolution enumerated twenty crimes punishable with death;

[16]

in Virginia and Kentucky there were twenty-seven. Modern legislation recognizes the futility as well as the fundamental injustice of such crass and indiscriminate retribution, and reserves the final penalty for the supreme crime against the life of the individual or the State.

At the same time there has been a twofold rectification of the scope of the criminal law. Some of the offences most severely punished in old times have ceased to be grounds of prosecution: for example, heresy, witchcraft, religious nonconformity. On the other hand, misdeeds which formerly were disregarded have been made punishable. It was not until 1833 that the English law began to treat drunkenness as a crime, rather than a misfortune. In 1857 a fraud on the part of a trustee, and in 1875 the falsification of accounts, were declared to be criminal. The laws of various States are recognizing and defining a vast number of new misdemeanors, such as the adulteration of foods, gambling, violation of laws in restraint of the liquor traffic, selling cigarettes to children, tapping electric wires, disfiguring the landscape with advertisements or printing them on the American flag, making combinations in restraint of trade, sleeping in a public bakery, spitting on the floor of a street-car. I do not say that all of these offences are wisely defined or fairly punished; but I do say that the process of modern legislation in regard to such matters indicates a growing desire among men that justice shall prevail in the community.

A large part of what appears to be the increase of crime in recent years (according to statistics), is due to this new definition of misdemeanors. There are more offenders in the most peaceful and well-governed States, because there are more offences defined. Another part comes from the greater efficiency in the execution of laws and the greater completeness in the tabulation of reports. The remaining part comes from a cause on which I will touch later. But in spite of this apparent increase of crime, no sensible man believes that the actual amount of violence and disorder among men is as great as it used to be. Pike's "History of Crime in England" estimates that in the fourteenth century murders were at least sixteen times as frequent as in our own day.

I pass by such notorious and splendid triumphs of the world's moral sense as the abolition of the slave-trade, and the establishment of international law, to mention two humble, concrete illustrations of what I mean by the advance of justice. The purchase by the American Government of the lands of the Spanish friars in the Philippines was a just way of accomplishing what would have been done a century ago by confiscation. The passage by the Congress of the United States of an act granting copyright to foreigners was a recognition, resisted by selfishness and ignorance for fifty years, of the fundamental principles of righteousness and fair dealing.

I know there are many items, and some of them most grievous, to be set down on the other side. There are still wars of conquest; corruptions and delays in legislation; oppressions and inequalities in government; robberies and cruelties which go unpunished. But these are not new things: they are as old as sin; evils not yet shaken off. I do not dream that the world is already quite just. But by the light that comes from the wiser, fairer laws of many lands, I guess that the world is growing more just.

In regard to the increase of kindness in the human race, the evidence is even more clear and strong. There are more people in the world who love mercy, and they are having better success in making their spirit prevail. More is being done to-day to prevent and mitigate human suffering, to shelter and protect the weak and helpless, to minister wisely to the sick and wounded in body and in mind, than ever before in the history of mankind. Part of the evidence of this lies in some of the facts already noted in connection with the humanizing of the law, and in the extraordinary story of the work begun by John Howard, a hundred and thirty years ago, which has cleansed away so much of the shame of a cruel, filthy, and irrational prison-system. But there is evidence, also, of a more direct and positive sort, going beyond the removal of ancient evils and manifesting a spirit of creative kindness eager to find new ways of helping others.

Since the middle of the nineteenth century, says the best authority on statistics, charity has grown twice as fast as wealth in England, three times as fast in France. In the United States the amount of the larger gifts ($5,000 or more) rose from $29,000,000, in 1893, to $107,000,000, in 1901. The public and private charities of New York alone (excluding the money spent on buildings) are estimated at $50,000,000 a year.

With all this increase of money comes an equal increase of care and thought in regard to the best way of using it for the real benefit of mankind. Reckless almsgiving is recognized as an amiable but idiotic form of self-indulgence. The penny dropped into the beggar's hat gives place to an inquiry into the beggar's condition. This costs more, but it is worth more. Waste in money given is no more virtuous than waste in money earned. Schools of philanthropy are established to study and teach the economy of generosity. Asylums are investigated and supervised. Relief funds are intrusted to responsible committees, who keep books and render accounts. Men and women are trying to take the head into partnership with the heart in beneficence. A rich father and mother lose their child by scarlet fever: they give a million dollars to endow an institution for the study and prevention of infectious diseases. An excursion steamboat is burned in New York harbor and a thousand people, most of them poor, lose their lives: within two weeks $125,-000 is given for relief; it is not thrown away with open hands, but administered by a committee with as much care as they would bestow on their own affairs; every dollar is accounted for, and a balance of $17,000 is left, to meet future calls, or to be devoted to some kindred purpose. These are illustrations of intelligent mercy.

Consider the advance in the general spirit of kindness which is indicated by such a fact as the founding and successful operation of the system of Working Men's Insurance in Germany. A certain sum of money is set aside for each workman every week (the employer and the employee each contributing half), and the Government adds a supplement of $12 on each pension. Ten million workmen are thus insured against sickness; seventeen million against accident; ten million against disability from old age. Six hundred and seventy thousand persons receive the benefit of this fund in yearly pensions. Incidentally there has been an immense benefit in the increase of precautions to prevent accidents and to reduce dangerous occupations. The employer who is not yet willing to protect his workmen, for kindness' sake, will do it to escape heavier taxes. And the community which silently compels him to do this, the community which says to the labouring man, "If you will perform your duty, you shall not starve when you are sick and old," is certainly growing more kind as well as more just.

Look at the broad field of what we may call international mercy. It has been estimated that since the days when the failure of the harvest drove Abraham from Palestine down to Egypt to seek food for his starving people, there have been three hundred and fifty great famines in various parts of the world. How many of the hungry nations received help from the outside world before the nineteenth century began? But now, within a week after the distress is known, money, food, and help of all kinds begin to flow in from all quarters of the globe. The famine in India in 1900–1901 called forth contributions from Great Britain, Germany, France, America, to the amount of $72,000,000. The greater part came from England, of course, but the whole world stood ready to aid her.

After the great fire of London in 1666, and the Lisbon earthquake in 1755, there was some outside assistance given, it is true. But in the main, the stricken cities had to suffer alone and help themselves. When the little city of Galveston, Texas, was swept by flood in 1900, within three weeks $750,000 was poured in for its relief, and the whole fund amounted to nearly a million and a half.

Turn again to look at the effort which the world is making to get rid of the hell of war, or, if that be not possible, at least to mitigate its horrors and torments. The High Tribunal of Arbitration at The Hague is a milestone on the world's path of progress toward the peaceful method of solving international disputes. Each year sees some new advance in that direction. Since 1903 Great Britain and France, Holland and Denmark, France and Spain, Great Britain and Italy, France and Holland, Great Britain and Spain,

Italy and France, have made treaties by which they pledge themselves to refer all differences of certain kinds which may arise between them to this tribunal for settlement. During the same time at least seven international questions have been referred to special arbitrators.

True, war has not yet been eliminated from the programme of the race. Great armaments are maintained at incredible expense, and nations insist, as Ruskin said, that it is good policy to purchase terror of one another at the cost of hundreds of millions every year. Some of the honest friends of peace are not yet reasonable enough to see the folly of this arrangement. A peace which depends upon fear is nothing but a suppressed war. Every now and then the restraining fear gives way, in one place or another, and thousands of men are

[28]

dressed in uniform and marshalled with music to blow one another's brains out.

But, in spite of all this, the growth of the spirit of mercy in the world makes itself known in the application of more humane rules to the inhumanity of war. Private wars, prevalent in the Middle Ages, and piracy, tolerated until the nineteenth century, have been abolished. The slaughter, torture, and enslavement of prisoners of war, which was formerly practised by even Christian nations, gave place in the middle of the seventeenth century to the custom of releasing all prisoners at the close of the war without ransom. Even Mahometan nations agreed by treaty that they would no longer subject their captives to bondage or torture. Persia and Turkey, in 1828, pledged themselves to the exchange of prisoners.

There has been a steady advance in

the strictness and efficiency of the rules
protecting the life and property of non-
combatants, an immense decrease in the
atrocities inflicted by conquering armies
upon the peaceful inhabitants of van-
quished countries. Let any man read
the story of the siege and sack of a town
in Holland by the Spanish soldiers as
it is given in Motley's "Dutch Republic," and compare it with the story
of the capture of Paris in 1870, or even
the taking of Pekin in 1900, and he will
understand that war itself has felt the
restraining touch of mercy. Let him reflect upon the significance of the work
of the Red Cross Society, with its
pledge of kindly succor to all who are
wounded in battle, "treating friend and
foe alike"; let him consider the remark-
able fact that this society in Japan has
a service as perfectly organized as any
in the world, with a million members,

and an annual income of more than
$1,500,000, and he cannot but acknowl-
edge that the spirit of pity and compassion has gained ground since the days
of Charlemagne and Barbarossa and
Napoleon—yes, even since the days of
Libby Prison and Elmira. And if none
of these things are enough to comfort
or encourage him, let him take in the
meaning of the simple fact that not one
of the great nations of the world to-day
would dare to proclaim a war in the
name of Religion. By this blessed
change alone, I should make bold to
guess that the world is surely growing
better.

But how is it with the third factor
of real betterment: self-restraint, the
willingness to sacrifice one's own passion and pleasure for the good of
others? Here, I confess, my guessing is
confused and troubled. There was a

vast improvement from the fourteenth to the nineteenth century, no doubt. But whether the twentieth century is carrying on the advance seems uncertain.

It may be that on this point we have entered into a period of reaction. The theory of individual liberty threatens to assert itself in dangerous forms. Literature and art are throwing their enchantments about the old lie that life's highest value is found in moments of intense self-gratification. Speed is glorified, regardless of direction. Strength is worshipped at the expense of reason. Success is deified as the power to do what one likes. Gilding covers a multitude of sins.

On the one hand, we have a so-called "upper class," which says: "The world was made to amuse me; nothing else matters." On the other hand, we have

[32]

an apparent increase of the criminal class, which lives at war with the social order. Corporations and labour unions engage in a struggle so fierce that the rights and interests of the community are forgotten by both parties. In our own country lynching, which is organized murder for unproved offences, grows more common; divorces increase to 60,000 in one year; and there is an epidemic of shocking accidents and disasters, greater than any hitherto recorded, and due apparently to the spirit of unrestraint and recklessness which is sweeping furiously in its motor-car along the highways of modern life.

Is this selfish and headlong spirit growing? Will it continue to accelerate the pace at which men live, and diminish the control by which they are guided? Will it weaken more and more the bonds of reverence, and mutual consideration, and household fidelity, and civic virtue, until the states which have been civilized by the sanctions of love and the convictions of duty are whirled backward, by the passion of self-indulgence, into the barbarism of luxurious pleasure or the anarchy of social strife?

These are the questions that rise to trouble us in our moments of despondency and foreboding. But I think that it is neither wise nor brave to give them an answer of despair. Two are stronger than one. The growth of justice and of kindness, I guess, will in the long run prevail over the decline of self-restraint, and the selfish, reckless spirit will be overcome.

At all events, when Christmas comes I shall sit down with John Friendly to enjoy its cheer, rather than with any sour pessimist. For one thing is sure. The hope of humanity lies in the widening, deepening influence of that blessed Life which was born nineteen hundred years ago in Bethlehem. The Lesson which that Life teaches us is that the only way to make the world better is for each man to do his best.

II

RULING CLASSES IN A DEMOCRACY

A DEMOCRACY differs from a monarchy, an empire, an aristocracy, not in the absence of ruling classes, but in the method by which they are selected.

Government without rulers is as impossible as steering without rudders. Man is by nature a civil creature. His natural rights, however you may define them, coexist with a natural instinct of organization. Organization implies order. Order implies control. Control implies authority. Authority implies a ruling class.

Rudiments of this civil instinct may be seen in some of the lower animals.

Bees and ants reflect, in a dim and partial way, the image of an organized state. Herds of elephants and horses, colonies of birds and beavers, are obedient to leadership and direction. In almost every case we can measure a creature's place in the scale of intelligence by the force and efficiency of the civil instinct. Man is no exception, but the great example. The first social problem is the problem of rule: who shall exercise it, how far shall it go, and by what means shall it be enforced? The highest social triumph is the establishment of authority in the hands of those who are best fitted to exercise it.

But while man has an instinct which recognizes and seeks this end, he has also an impulse which rebels against the means necessary to secure it. The freedom of the will carries with it the craving for unrestrained liberty of action.

[37]

But liberty absolutely unrestrained is inconsistent with the existence of any kind of rule.

Suppose that you and I are farmers, whose fields march together. If you are free to do just what you please, and I am free to do precisely what I like, it is not probable that peace will prevail along our line-fences; at least not until we are both perfectly sanctified and the millennium arrives, which is evidently some distance away. Meantime it is quite necessary for both of us that there should be some one authorized and competent to say what shall be done about those line-fences; and how the roads which we use in common shall be kept up; and how the agreements which we make to exchange our labour, or the products of our labour, shall be enforced; and what means shall be used to guard us both against common dangers and disasters; and how the cost of these things shall be divided.

This is rule. The men who have "the say" about these subjects belong to the ruling classes. Against them, and against the things that they say, the impulse of unregulated freedom always reluctates.

Few men doubt their ability to make laws. Most men, at some time or other, dislike the necessity of obeying them. Personal restraints are not often personal pleasures. The visit of the tax-collector seldom gives unmixed joy. It is easier to do what you please than to do what you ought. Individual rights seem more concrete and familiar than reciprocal duties. Under every form of government known to man there has been, there still is, and there probably will be, an element of discontent and restlessness arising from the natural human impulse—natural at least to man in his present condition—to resist rule.

The problem of civilization is how to subdue this impulse by correlating individual rights with social duties, and how to develop, enlighten, and guide the civil instinct which seeks order through rule.

Now, it is evident that the method of selecting the ruling classes must have a considerable influence in the working out of this problem. It is true that at any given time people are most likely to be contented, peaceful, and happy under the rulers who actually give them the most firm, orderly, and equitable government, no matter how they may have been selected. There is a certain amount of hard common sense in the remark of Alexander Pope, although it was made in verse:

"For forms of government let fools contest;
  Whate'er is best administered is best."

But the wisdom of this couplet is confined to the present tense. It is good only for the moment in which it is uttered. A form of government may be well administered to-day, badly to-morrow. The great question is, how to secure a continuity of good administration. How shall the men who are best qualified to control and direct the common interests of their fellow-men be discovered? How shall they be sanctioned in the use of just authority, and restrained from the exercise of unjust tyranny? How shall it be made most easy to correct the accident of power falling into unfit hands? How shall the great force of public opinion, from which, in the last analysis, all governments derive their energy and stability —how shall this common sense of jus-

[41]

tice and right be satisfied in the selection of the ruling class?

Different methods have been devised. They may be classed under three heads: autocratic, automatic, and democratic.

The autocratic method practically amounts to allowing the chief ruler to select himself and appoint his subordinates. This is the oldest method and the rudest—

> "the simple plan
> That those should take who have the power,
> And those should keep who can."

It is based upon the assumption that might coincides with right. This would be convenient if it were true. It would be a great saving of time if we could just let the strongest man rule, and feel sure that he was the best. But, unfortunately, the history of imperial sway does not support this idea. When an autocrat imposes the taxes, there is often "the de'il to pay." And when a tyrant chooses the judges, Justice does not need to have her eyes bandaged, for she is stone-blind already.

The automatic method relies upon heredity to supply the ruling classes. Certain families are endowed with titles and powers, and the head of a particular family inherits the sovereignty. All that he has to do is to be born at the right time, and live long enough, and the sceptre comes to him as a matter of course. Meantime natural forces are at work producing hereditary legislators to support and share his power. The scheme has an aspect of antique dignity and piety. It appears to put great reliance upon Providence, and, indeed, it has often sanctioned itself in old times by an appeal to the "Divine Right of Kings." In practice it has two very serious drawbacks. First, the wrong family may be chosen to start the procession; and, second, the so-called law of heredity often produces very unexpected and curious results.

The democratic method intrusts the selection of the ruling classes to the collective reason and justice of the people. In the conduct of government it appeals to the governed for their consent. "Consent of the governed," in this connection, does not mean their permission, merely; for if this were the meaning, it would be equally true of a constitutional monarchy, and even of a benevolent and popular empire. The subjects of Edward VII. and of William II. "consent," in this sense, to their governments, with practically as much unanimity as the citizens of the United States feel at any given time in consenting to the authority of the President in office. The "consent" of democracy, if it has any distinctive meaning, must signify the thinking together, the acting together, of the people in the choice of their rulers, and, consequently, in the direction of the state. Three things are essential to the reality of this popular participation.

First, there must be an untrammelled opportunity for the people to express their choice by suffrage. It is by no means necessary that this suffrage should be universal. As a matter of fact, it never has been. There is no nation known to history in which all citizens, male and female, old and young, native and foreign-born, have had the suffrage. It is not a common right. It is a civil privilege intended to protect common rights. It has always been restricted in one way or another. The only things necessary to its sufficiency are that it should be truly representative,

[45]

and that the conditions which restrict it should be equal for all, except in the case of forfeiture for crime.

The second essential of popular participation in government is that the terms of office of those who are chosen to rule should be so limited that changes of national judgment, arising from experience, from education, or from changed circumstances, may be made effective without rebellion or revolution.

The third essential is that the functions and powers of the ruling classes thus chosen should be restricted to those which are actually conferred in the choice. For this reason there can be no real and permanent democracy without a constitution. True democrats are jealous and zealous for the sanctity of the constitution. They know that it is the sea-wall between them and autocracy.

Now, where these three essentials exist,—a representative and equal suffrage, periodical opportunity for the people to change their rulers peacefully, and a careful limitation of official powers by the constitution,—there is genuine democracy.

Foreign critics say that the United States is not a truly democratic country, because the people are not all on a level, all alike. But when did democracy offer to guarantee the similarity of people, or grade mankind down to a dead flat? When all the trees in the forest have the same number of leaves, when all the rivers that flow into the sea contain the same number of fish, when all the fields in the farm bear the same crop, then will all men be alike in their power and skill, and consequently on a level in degree and station. Democracy is no miracle-worker, no infidel toward natural law. Democracy declares that men, unequal in their endowments, shall be equal in their rights to develop those endowments.

Classes must exist in every social order —ruling classes, teaching classes, agricultural classes, manufacturing classes, commercial classes. All these are in the labouring class, but their labour is divided. The moment you begin to divide labour you begin to differentiate men. The moment you have men developed, by different kinds of work, on different sides of their nature, you have classes.

What democracy says is that there shall be no locked doors between these classes. Every stairway shall be open. Every opportunity shall be free. Every talent shall have an equal chance to earn another talent. I think we may claim that this is the case in the United States, at least to a larger extent than ever before in the history of the world. Not all the farmers' boys in the country may become Presidents of the nation. That would be physically impossible. But any of them may do so, and several of them have done so. Some of them, like Henry Clay and Daniel Webster, attained such eminence and power that the Presidency could hardly have added to their fame.

These cases are not accidents. They are logical evidences of an equality among men in the only sense in which equality is possible—equality of opportunity. This equality is no nebulous dream of a state in which degree is abolished and every man is as mediocre as everybody else. It is a real escape from the tyranny of artificial and hereditary distinctions; a real approximation of position and fitness, honour and ability. It is safeguarded, and its effects are diffused in some measure through the whole fabric of social life, not by any mere legal enactment, but by something vastly stronger and more efficient: the state of mind which is created in the people by committing to them the choice of their own ruling classes. Herein is fulfilled the divine prophecy of democracy: "And their nobles shall be of themselves, and their governors shall proceed from the midst of them."

In regard to this democratic method of electing rulers there are some things which I should like to say, with as much emphasis and clearness as may be consistent with brevity.

It is the highest and most reasonable method. In the case of ignorant, undeveloped peoples, with whom the impulse of resistance is stronger than the instinct of order, the other methods may be necessary. But they are to be considered as educative, corrective, disciplinary. All peoples, like all children, should be regarded as on their way to self-rule. When they are able to maintain it, they are entitled to have it. All arguments against the democratic method, based on the weakness, folly, and selfishness of human nature, apply with greater force to the autocratic and automatic methods. The individual follies of a multitude of men often neutralize one another, leaving an active residuum of plain common sense. But for a fool king there is no natural antidote; and sometimes men have sadly found that the only way to set his head straight was to remove it.

It is said that democracies are peculiarly subject to the microbes of financial delusion and the resultant boom-fever and panic-chill. But the Mississippi

Scheme and the South Sea Bubble flourished under monarchical institutions; and the worst-depreciated currencies in the world have been stamped with the image and superscription of kings.

It is said that democracies are reckless, extravagant, spendthrift, and that official dishonesty and corruption thrive in them. But it would be difficult to parallel the extravagance and corruption of the government of France under the Bourbons, in the history of any republic. The Russian railway across Siberia has been built through a quagmire of public peculation as vast as the Empire itself. And when the records of South Africa are fully written, unless all signs fail, it will be found that the pickings of the rulers of the Boer republics, compared with those of the servants of the new British Overlord of the Transvaal, were on the scale of one horse to a thousand mules.

It is said that democracies sometimes choose weak, incompetent, and even bad men for their ruling classes. So they do. But they have no monopoly in this respect. The automatic method of selecting rulers produced Charles II. and James II. and George III. It would be difficult to surpass in any republic the folly which selected Lord North to guide the policy of Great Britain at a time when Lord Chatham, Charles James Fox, and Edmund Burke were on the stage. Yet this was done, not by an ignorant democracy, but by an automatic king. Nor does the autocratic plan of allowing rulers to choose themselves work any more infallibly. France had two examples of it in the last century. Napoleon I. was a catastrophe. Napoleon III. was a crime.

[53]

All that may be said of the propriety of appealing to Providence and trusting God for the ordaining of the powers that be, applies to the democratic method even more than to any other. Why should we suppose that Providence has anything more to do with the ambition of a strong man to climb a throne, than with the desire of a great people to make a strong man their leader? Why should we imagine that God is any more willing to direct the intricacies of royal marriages, and regulate the matrimonial alliances of titled personages, for the sake of producing proper kings and lords, than to guide the thoughts and desires of a great people and turn their hearts to the choice of good presidents? The characteristic of democracy, says James Russell Lowell, is its habit of "asking the Powers that Be, at the most inconvenient moment, whether they are the Powers that Ought to Be." And what is this question but an appeal to the divine judgment and law?

There is as much room for Providence to act in the growth of public opinion as in the rise and propagation of a royal house. What royal house is there that goes so far to vindicate the ways of God to man as the succession of Presidents chosen by the people of the American Republic? Some of the choices have not been brilliant, a few have been unfortunate, none has been evil or corrupt. There is no line of hereditary kings, no line of autocratic emperors, that claims as many great men, or half as many good men, in an equal period of time, as the line of Presidents of the United States.

There is warrant, then, in reason and in experience, for believing in the divine

[55]

right of democracy. It is not the only righteous and lawful method of selecting rulers, but it is the highest and most reasonable. We lift our patriotism above the shallow and flashy enthusiasm for institutions merely because they are ours. We confide ourselves to the hopeful and progressive view of human nature, to the faith that God is able to make truth and right reason prevail in the arena of public opinion. We bless the memory of our first and greatest hero because he had no desire for a crown, and so, by his personal influence, helped to make the choice of ruling classes in the United States neither autocratic nor automatic, but democratic.

But this method of providing for civil rule has its dangers, which cannot be denied, and which ought not to be forgotten.

Government by majority is not an infallible device for securing the best wisdom at any particular moment. It is a good working plan for conducting the experiments which need to be tried in order to determine, by success or failure, the direction in which the best wisdom lies. Our local failures ought to be as instructive as our general success. In our prosperity we should imitate the custom of the Romans, who sobered the joys of a public triumph by the presence of a monitor to warn the victor that he was not exempt from the dangers and frailties of mortality.

Three chief perils attend the democratic method of selecting the ruling classes:

The red peril of the rise of the demagogue.

The yellow peril of the dominance of wealth.

The black peril of the rule of the Boss.

There is a singular relationship among these perils. They are interwoven and concomitant. Unlike as are the men in whom they are separately embodied, the man through whom they all become possible is one and the same:—the celebrated "man with the hoe."

Hear a parable of the machine, the money-bag, the mouth, and the hoe. The man with the machine persuaded the man with the hoe to vote precisely according to orders, and thus made himself of much value as an agent of barter or an instrument of assessment. The man with the money-bag, desiring protection or power, went into the marketplace and found there the man with the machine, whereupon these two discovered a community of interest. This worked well until the man with the hoe grew suspicious that his part in the transaction, while the most important, was the least profitable. Then appeared the man with the mouth, promising to wind up the concern, distribute the assets, and alter the laws of nature so far as necessary to effect a universal exchange of hoes for money-bags. This programme was not fully carried out. But the machine was put temporarily out of repair; the money-bag was sent abroad for its health; the mouth had an opportunity to explain some of its promises and retract the rest; and the hoe, having marched in several processions and gained much experience, went on hoeing as before.

I do not mean to say that this somewhat allegorical description has ever been completely realized, on any large scale in our country. But certain fragmentary features of it may be dimly recognized, here and there, in our politics. Men whose chief distinction is their wealth, men whose only profession is the manipulation of political wires, (underground,) men who are related to real statesmen as quacks to real physicians, have at times found their way into our ruling classes. Their presence is a menace to the integrity and security of the democracy.

Legislation hostile to wealth is political brigandage. Legislation subservient to wealth is political suicide. It cannot be denied that "money talks." The thing to be prevented is that money should talk with more tongues than belong to it, and that it should say things that are neither true nor just, and that these things should be made laws for the people.

It is not likely that rich men, by virtue of their riches, will ever become the ruling class in this country, in the open. The natural operation of jealousy and envy will take care of that. The possession of a large estate, in the eyes of those who do not consider how it was acquired nor how it is used, will always be a cause of suspicion, often, as in the case of Washington, most ungenerous and unjust. But that rich men should endeavor to control legislation, local and national, in their own interest, and to secure influence and thus to become a ruling class in secret, is more than likely. It is natural. It is a fact.

But what makes it possible in a democracy? No one could buy a vote if someone else were not willing to sell a vote. No one could run a legislature from his office if there were not a lobby at the capitol. No lobby could do business if there were not a machine. And no machine can fulfil the law of its own

[61]

being without evolving a Boss. Here
is the law of development of this species of political creature: First a society; then a faction; then a gang; then
a clique; then a ring; then a Big Four,
or Five, or Six; then a Boss.

There are States in this country where
a single man has owned virtually all
the places, from the mayoralty of the
biggest town down to the postmaster-
ship of the smallest village. There are
cities in this country where the public
franchises, the public pay-roll, and the
public offices have been for years practically under the control of a secret society, and this secret society under control of a chief as autocratic as Rob Roy
or Robin Hood. This is a ruling class
with a vengeance. This is democracy
deformed.

It would not be so bad, perhaps, if it
were an intelligent, benevolent, public-

spirited despotism. But, usually, this kind of rule is marked by shrewd ignorance, crass selfishness, bold dishonesty. Its dark consummate flower was William M. Tweed, of New York, who reigned over the city for seven years; stole $6,000,000 or more for himself, and $60,000,000 or more for his followers; was indorsed at the height of his corruption by six of the richest citizens of the metropolis; had a public statue offered to him by *The New York Sun* as a "noble benefactor of the city"; and summed up his career, at the time of his commitment to the penitentiary, in the following conversation with the warden:

"What is your occupation?" "Statesman."

"What is your religion?" "None."

It is an error to assume, and a crime to assert, that rulers of this type are

common in our country. The Tweeds
are not normal; they are exceptional.
They have not yet become endemic,
though in certain localities they seem
almost epidemic. They have not in-
fected the higher levels of national government, but they have sometimes made
themselves felt there. And their presence, the power that they wield through
the poor man whom they cajole and deceive, and through the rich man whom
they threaten and serve, the possibilities
of wider and deeper corruption which
they suggest, ought to remind us that
the democratic method of selecting rulers, although, (or perhaps because,) it
is the highest and most reasonable,
needs to be all the more closely watched,
safeguarded, and defended against its
own inherent dangers.

What, then, is the safeguard of democracy in the choice of the ruling

classes? We have certainly put all our eggs into the basket of popular suffrage. How shall we watch and protect that basket?

Education is the only possible safeguard which is in harmony with our principles and has the power to defend our institutions without enslaving them. I know not how this truth could be expressed more lucidly than it was stated in the charter of the University of Georgia in 1785:

As it is the distinguishing happiness of her governments that civil order should be the result of choice and not of necessity, and the common wishes of the people become the law of the land, their public prosperity and even existence very much depend upon suitably forming the minds and morals of their citizens. . . . This is an influence beyond the reach of laws and punishments, and can be claimed only by religion and education.

"Platitudes!" some votary of novelty exclaims. Then so are virtue and honour and patriotism platitudes. It is by forgetting platitudes that men and nations are ruined. Platitudes are truths that are flat, level, and therefore fitted to use as foundations. It is by building on such foundations that social and political fabrics are made firm, square, and enduring.

"The first need of our country," said Lord Rosebery in his Rectorial Address before the University of Glasgow in 1900, "is the want of men. We want men for all sorts of high positions—first-rate men, if possible; if not, as nearly first-rate as may be."

But what means of producing first-rate men has been discovered, except education? I do not mean that kind of education which adorns a chosen few with the tinsel gewgaws of useless accomplishments. I mean that nobler education which aims to draw out and discipline all that is best in manhood—to make the mind clear and firm by study, the body strong and obedient by exercise, the moral sense confident and inflexible by disclosing the eternal principles upon which it rests.

What means except education can produce that other kind of men, whom Lord Rosebery did not mention, but who are no less essential to the welfare of a democracy—men who are capable of recognizing first-rate men, and choosing them for the ruling classes?

It is of little use for a republic to have higher institutions of learning producing men of wisdom and power, unless it has also a system of general, nay, of universal, education producing popular respect for humane wisdom and righteous power. The university at the summit, reaching as high as human intelligence can go, the common school at the basis, spreading as wide as human nature itself, and between them the best attainable system of grammar schools and high schools and academies, and branching out from them an ever-developing organization of technical and professional institutions—these are the defences of the republic.

It was the opinion of Thomas Jefferson that the best service he rendered to his countrymen was in the thought which he gave to the unfolding of this doctrine, and the work which he did to put it into practice in Virginia. Certainly there was no other way in which he showed more truly that he was a democrat.

Suppose, for example, that we are compelled to meet practically one of the dangers which are inherent in government by democracy. Suppose that by the extension of the suffrage the power of choosing rulers has come into the hands of a mass of ignorant voters like the negroes in some of the Southern States. They are coherent in their action, because they are bound together by racial and social ties; incoherent in their judgment, because their only real unity lies in the absence of knowledge and fixed principle. This coherent mass of incoherency, like a cargo of loose wheat in the hold of a ship, will imperil the equilibrium of the state in every hour of storm and stress.

The privilege of suffrage bestowed on ignorance is not a protection of natural rights; it is a detriment to them. It is like a diamond hung around the neck of a child, an invitation to kidnappers; like a can of dynamite in the hands of a fool, a prophecy of explosion. But how is the difficulty to be removed, the danger to be averted? Only two methods are possible: the restriction of the suffrage: the education of the ignorant.

The restriction of the suffrage is a temporary expedient. It may be wise, it may even be indispensable under certain conditions. Certainly there can be no objection to it, if it be accomplished through laws which are alike for all and uncoloured by prejudice. But at best it goes no further than that process which physicians call the encystment of a tumour. It shuts the evil up in a sac, but does not take it away. The man who does not know enough to be trusted with a vote can never be a pleasant or a safe neighbour. The man who is too ignorant to choose his own rulers will never be an easy citizen for anyone to rule.

But education, though a slow remedy, is thorough-going. It reaches the root of the disease. Wisdom and justice alike demand that the permanent cure should be used even while the temporary palliative is applied. A wise and loyal democracy will never restrict the suffrage by an educational qualification, without providing, at the same time, the educational privileges which will give all its citizens an opportunity to rise above the level of the restriction.

The amount of money to be expended by a democracy in public education is to be measured by the standard of intelligent manhood which it sets for its citizens. The standard, I say, for, after all, in these matters it is the silent ideal in the hearts of the people which moulds character and guides action. What is your ideal of a right American? The answer to that question will determine whether you think we ought to do more or less for popular education.

For my part, I reckon that, as the enlightenment and discipline of manhood is the best safeguard of a democracy, so it ought to be the object of our chief care and our largest expenditure.

If our naval and military expenses ever surpass or even equal our educational expenses, we shall be on the wrong track. If we ever put the fortress and the fleet above, or even on a level with, the schoolhouse and the university, our sense of perspective will be out of focus. If we ever spend more to inspire awe and fear in other peoples than to cultivate intelligence and character in our own, we shall be on the road to the worst kind of bankruptcy, —a bankruptcy of men.

We want the common school more generously supported and more intelligently directed, so that the power to read and think shall become the property of all, and so that the principles

[72]

of morality, which must be based on religion, shall be taught to every American child. We want the door between the common school and the university wide open, so that the path which leads upward from the little red schoolhouse to the highest temple of learning shall be free, and the path that leads downward from academic halls to the lowliest dwelling and workshop of instruction shall be honourable. We want a community of interest and a cooperation of forces between the public-school teacher and the college faculty. We want academic freedom, so that the institutions of learning may be free from all suspicion of secret control by the money-bag or the machine. We want democratic universities, where a man is honoured only for what he is and what he knows. We want American education, so that every citizen shall not only

believe in democracy, but know what it
means, what it costs, and what it is
worth.

"O thronèd Freedom, unto thee is brought
    Empire; nor falsehood, nor blood-payment
      asked;
Who never through deceit thine ends hast
      sought,
    Nor toiling millions for ambition tasked;
Unlike the fools who build the throne
    Of fraud and wrong and woe;
For man at last will take his own,
    Nor count the overthrow;
But far from these is set thy continent,
    Nor fears the Revolution in man's rise;
On laws that with the weal of all consent,
    And saving truths that make the people wise.
For thou art founded in the eternal fact
That every man doth greaten with the act
Of freedom; and doth strengthen with the
    weight
Of duty; and diviner moulds his fate,
By sharp experience taught the thing he lacked,
God's pupil; thy large maxim framed, though
    late,
Who masters best himself best serves the
    State."

[74]

III

PUBLICOMANIA

IT is a strange thing to see how deeply certain people of our time have been smitten with a form of insanity which we may call, for want of a dictionary word, publicomania. The name is rather ugly, and altogether irregular, being of mixed Latin and Greek descent. But it is no worse than the thing it describes, which is, in fact, a sort of mongrel madness. It has some kinship with the Roman Grandio's passion for celebrity which Seneca satirized, and not a little likeness to the petty ostentation of Beau Tibbs at which Goldsmith laughed kindly in London a century ago.

But in our own day the disease has developed a new symptom. It is not enough to be pointed out with the forefinger of notoriety: the finger which points must be stained with printer's ink. The craving for publicity is not satisfied with anything but a paragraph in the newspapers; then it wants a column; and finally it demands a whole page with illustrations. The delusion consists in the idea that a sufficient quantity of this kind of notoriety amounts to fame.

It is astonishing to observe how much time, ingenuity, money, and vital energy, people who are otherwise quite sane, will spend for the sake of having their names and unimportant doings chronicled, in a form of print which can be preserved only in private and very inconvenient scrap-books. In England, where they have a hereditary aristocracy

and a *Court Journal,* the mania seems
less difficult to understand. But in this
country, where the limits of the "smart
set" are confessedly undefined and inde-
finable, changing with the fluctuations
of the stock-market and the rise and fall
of real estate, it is impossible to conceive what benefit or satisfaction reasonable beings can derive from a temporary enrolment among the assistants
at fashionable weddings, the guests at
luxurious banquets, or the mourners at
magnificent funerals.

Our wonder increases when we consider that there is hardly a detail of private life, from the cradle to the grave,
which is not now regarded as appropri-
ate for publication, provided only the
newspapers are induced to take an interest in it. The interest of the public is
taken for granted. Formerly the intru-
sion of reporters into such affairs was

resented. Now it is their occasional neglect to intrude which causes chagrin.

If we could suppose that all this was only a subtle and highly refined mode of advertisement, it would be comparatively easy to account for it. There would be method in the madness. But why in the world should a man or a woman care to advertise things which are not to be sold—a wedding trousseau, the decorations of a bedroom, a dinner to friends, or the flowers which conceal a coffin? We can see well enough why a dealer in old silver should be pleased at having his wares described in the newspapers. But what interest has Mr. Newman Biggs in having the public made aware of the splendour and solidity of his plate?

Of course one must recognize that there is such a thing as public life. It is natural and reasonable that those who

are engaged in it should accept publicity, and even seek it within proper limits, so far as it may be a necessary condition of success in their work. Authors
and artists wish to have their books read
and their pictures looked at. Statesmen
and reformers desire to have their poli-
cies and principles discussed, in order
that they may be adopted. Benefactors
of mankind wish at least to have their
schools and hospitals and libraries received with as much attention as may
be needed to make them useful.

But why the people who are chiefly
occupied in eating and drinking, mar-
rying and giving in marriage, should
wish to have their lives turned inside
out on the news-stands passes comprehension. They subject themselves to all
the inconveniences of royalty (being, as
Montaigne says, "in all the daily actions of life encircled and hemmed in

by an importunate and tedious multitude"), without any of its compensa-
tions. They are exposed by their own
fantastic choice to what Cowley called
"a quotidian ague of frigid imperti-
nences," and they get nothing for it
but the disadvantage of being talked
about. The result of their labours and
sufferings is simply to bring them to
the condition of a certain Dr. William
Kenrick, of whom old Samuel Johnson
said, "Sir, he is one of those who have
made themselves public without making themselves known."

But if we are inclined to be scornful
of the vagaries of publicomania, this
feeling must surely be softened into
something milder and more humane
when we reflect upon the unhappy state
of mind to which it reduces those who
are afflicted with it. They are not as
other men, to whom life is sweet for its

own sake. The feasts to which they are
bidden leave them hungry unless their
presence is recorded in the *Daily Eaves-
dropper*. They are restless in their
summer rest unless their comings and
goings are printed in the chronicle
of fashionable intelligence. Their new
houses do not please them if the newspaper fails to give sufficient space to
the announcement that they are "at
home." It is a miserable condition, and
one from which all obscure and happy
persons should pray to be delivered.

There is, however, consolation for true
lovers of humanity in the thought that
the number of people who are afflicted
with this insanity in an incurable form
is comparatively small. They make a
great noise, like Edmund Burke's company of vociferous grasshoppers under
a leaf in the field where a thousand
cattle are quietly feeding; but, after

all, the great silent classes are in the
majority. The common sense of mankind agrees with the poet Horace in his
excellent praise of the joys of retire-
ment:

" Secretum iter, et fallentis semita vitæ."

One of the best antidotes and cures of
the craze for publicity is a love of
poetry and of the things that belong
to poetry—the beauty of nature, the
sweetness and splendour of the common human affections, and those high
thoughts and unselfish aspirations which
are the enduring treasures of the soul.
It is good to remember that the finest
and most beautiful things that can ever
come to us cannot possibly be news to
the public. It is good to find the zest of
life in that part of it which does not
need, and will not bear, to be advertised.
It is good to talk with our friends,

[82]

knowing that they will not report us;
and to play with the children, knowing
that no one is looking at us; and to eat
our meat with gladness and singleness
of heart. It is good to recognize that
the object of all true civilization is that
a man's house, rich or poor, shall be his
castle, and not his dime museum. It is
good to enter into the spirit of Wordsworth's noble sonnet, and, turning back
to "the good old cause," thank God for
those safeguards of the private life
which still preserve in many homes

> "Our peace, our fearful innocence,
> And pure religion breathing household laws."

IV

THE HERITAGE OF AMERI-CAN IDEALS

No banquet of an ancestral character can be held in the United States of America, whether under the banner of St. George, or of St. Nicholas, or of the uncanonized saints of Plymouth Rock, without a more or less oratorical recognition that our American stock is the product of a happy mixture.

The Puritan strain in our American social life is too well known to need description. Personal independence, religious intensity, ethical earnestness mitigated by commercial activity — this strain has made its mark deep on our American history.

The Dutch influence has not been so deep, but perhaps it has been broader. Free education and religious toleration came to this country from Holland. The Quakers could not live in the air of New England in the seventeenth century, but they found the atmosphere of New Amsterdam more hospitable. William Penn, who set the example of giving to the consciences of others the same freedom that he claimed for his own, had a Dutch mother. Religious liberty (which, take it all in all, is the most precious possession of America) is a watchword translated from the Dutch. It was William of Orange who put it in immortal language when he said, "Conscience is God's province."

The Cavalier influence has been a strain of grace, of dignity, of amenity; a sentiment of chivalry; a feeling of national pride and honour permeating all of our social life; and it has actually been one of the most powerful factors in consolidating the Republic. In the Federal Convention, "the Virginia plan" first held forth the idea of a strong nation as distinguished from a loose confederation. It was around the personal character of Washington that all the scattered forces of possible American citizenship first centred and crystallized. Without that great soldier-cavalier the Colonies hardly could have freed themselves; without that greater citizen-cavalier the States never could have united themselves.

The streams that have entered into our American life come from springs very wide apart—from the Puritans whom James I. was persecuting, and from the courtiers whom he was patronizing; from the Dutchmen whom

Charles II. was fighting, and from the Covenanters whom he was trying to convert at the pistol's point; from the Scotchmen who had captured the north of Ireland, and from the Huguenots who had been driven out of the south of France.

Yet with all these differences of ancestral stock, Americans have a common and undivided heritage of ancestral ideals. They are the fruits of that underlying unity of convictions, hopes, and purposes which made our forefathers one people. A love of liberty strong enough to harmonize different ways of conceiving it; a reverence for the rights of humanity deep enough to reconcile different ways of defending it; and a faith in God high enough to make room at last for all modes of expressing it—these essential qualities of manhood made the best men of the

Northern and the Middle and the Southern Colonies able to understand one another, and worked out through years of tribulation and triumph those inherited ideals which are the true riches and strength of America.

We have an inherited ideal of American manhood. We are not waiting for this ideal to arise; we are not expecting that it will be discovered and identified for us by any of those British authors who come over here looking for "the typical American." We do not even recognize it very clearly in Mr. Rudyard Kipling's extraordinary portrait:

" Enslaved, illogical, elate,
    He greets the embarrassed gods, nor fears
To shake the iron hand of fate,
    Or match with Destiny for beers.

" Lo, imperturbable he rules,
    Unkempt, disreputable, vast,
And in the teeth of all the schools
    I—I, shall save him at the last."

[88]

This verse, like much of Mr. Kipling's writing, has the charm of audacity, but it is hardly a happy description of our ancestral ideal of American manhood. We look back to that ideal as it was realized in the days of the Revolution, and we see that its typical representatives were neither enslaved nor illogical, neither unkempt nor disreputable. The men who made this country, and led it from the beginning, were men of intelligence as well as of independence, men of dignity as well as of daring, men of sobriety as well as of self-confidence. Lowell was wrong when he called Lincoln "the first American." Lincoln was a great, an unsurpassably great, American, but he was not the first. Washington, Franklin, Jay, Adams, Jefferson —these were all Americans before Lincoln.

The differences in manner, speech, and

dress among our ancestors do not obscure the fundamental resemblance of their manhood. Along the Yankee line we see such names as Hancock, Ellsworth, Sherman, Putnam, Greene, and Lincoln. Along the Cavalier line we trace the records of a Washington, a Madison, a Pinckney, a Randolph, a Lee. Along the Dutch line we see such men as Schuyler, Livingston, DeWitt Clinton, Van Buren. These men come of different stock, but they are not strangers, they are not aliens, they are of the same breed; and while that breed lasts we shall not need to ask any foreign critic to identify the typical American. He has arrived. He is no bully with his breeches tucked in his boots; he is no braggart with a wild, barbaric yawp. This typical American is a clear-eyed, level-headed, straightforward, educated, self-respecting gentleman with frank manners and firm convictions, who acts on the principle that—

> " The rank is but the guinea's stamp,
>   A man's a man, for a' that."

We have also inherited an ideal of American government. The men who met in Independence Hall in 1776 had a very distinct conviction in their minds, and they had the capacity to express it in clear language. They believed that "government derives its just powers from the consent of the governed." They believed that all men are born equal, not in personal gifts, but in their rights to life, liberty, and the pursuit of happiness. They believed that taxation without representation is not government, but tyranny; that the subjection of an unwilling people to foreign jurisdiction is tyranny; that the exaltation of the military over the civil power is tyranny. All these things they believed, and to maintain them they pledged their life, their property, and their sacred honour.

That proclamation heralded the birth of a new ideal of government. It contained three vital principles—free consent, equal rights, and legal self-control. It recognized in simple manhood, as Lowell so well said, "a certain privilege and adequacy," and it trusted manhood for the defence and development of its own rights. That was a daring trust— a trust which astounded the old world. Such an ideal of government involved not only an inspiration but also a restraint. When our forefathers adopted it, a little more than a hundred years ago, they knew that it involved a separation from the old world; but they regarded that separation as a benefit; they believed that as this new ideal of

[92]

government was separated from old ideals it would have a better chance to develop into something higher, purer, and stronger. They trusted that ideal well enough to follow it, believing that it would bring them prosperity, fame, and good renown. And so it did.

There are serious objections to such an ideal, of course. From the theoretical side, for instance, the famous historian Lecky tells us that democracy is a fallacy and that its failure will be proved. From the practical side a "statesman" like Mr. Cecil Rhodes tells us that if we wait for the consent of inferior races before we take possession of their territory, we shall miss the chance of trade. These objections, and others like them, have always been urged against the ideal of republicanism which was set forth by our ancestors. At times they have even seemed to produce a kind of

[93]

vacillation and weather-cockiness in certain sections of the public mind.

But, on the whole, the American people have followed, with a few inconsistencies, their inherited ideal of government with marvellous fidelity and still more marvelous success. Those inconsistencies were the cause of our most signal failures until we rectified them by emancipating the slaves and opening citizens' rights to the Indians.

There cannot possibly be any more optimistic view of the Republic to-day than that which recognizes in the triumphant success of our democracy the vindication of that ideal which was conceived by our ancestors. Without militarism it has made the power of America felt around the globe. Without colonies or dependencies it has enabled America to outstrip, in her export trade, the colonial empires. Without

[94]

conquering subject races America expanded her population, in a hundred years, from three millions to seventy-five millions.

The ideal of a nation conceived in liberty and dedicated to the proposition that all men are born with equal rights, is to-day the most potent and prosperous ideal in all the world. All that this country needs is to be true to it, and she will lead mankind for many centuries to come.

But was there an ideal of the future glory and world-power of America among those which we inherited? Did our forefathers know anything about it? Did it come within their horizon? There are those who tell us that the builders of the Republic were too short-sighted to behold this vision. We are asked to believe that their eyes were not opened in regard to the greatness of

America as a nation, and that therefore their counsels are inapplicable to the days of our prosperity. We are asked to believe that they did not dream of the future greatness of the country which they founded, otherwise they would have founded it differently. I do not believe it.

The representative of Spain at the Paris Convention in 1783, Count Aranda, wrote to his monarch, in regard to America, as follows: "This federal Republic is born a pygmy. The day will come when it will be a giant, a Colossus, formidable even in these countries. Liberty of conscience, the facility for establishing a new population on immense lands, as well as the advantages of a new governmnet, will draw thither farmers and artisans from all the nations." That was a Spanish vision of jealousy and fear. Is it likely that our forefathers were too blind to behold that same vision in joy and hope? No; they saw it, and they saw also how it would be realized. Not on the old plan of the Roman Empire, hitherto dominant throughout the world, that of annexation without incorporation; but on the new plan of the American Republic, the plan of liberation, education, assimilation.

Turn to the letter which Washington wrote to the Earl of Buchan: "It is my sincere wish that united America shall have nothing to do with the political intrigues or the squabbles of European nations. To administer justice and receive it from every power with whom they are connected will, I hope, be always found the most prominent feature of the administration of this country; and I flatter myself that nothing short of imperious necessity can ever occasion

[97]

a breach with any of them. Under such a system, if we are allowed to pursue it, the wealth of these United States, the agriculture, the mechanic arts, and the population will increase with that degree of rapidity as to baffle all calculation and must surpass any idea your Lordship can hitherto have entertained."

Turn to those noble words of the Farewell Address, in which the greatest American said: "It will be worthy of a free, enlightened, and at no distant period a great, nation to give to mankind the magnanimous and too novel example of a people always guided by an exalted sense of justice and benevolence." That is our ancestral ideal of national glory and expansion—not military conquest, but world-wide influence —not colonies in both hemispheres, but friends, admirers, and imitators around the globe—not a flag planted in whatever place the hand of power chooses to plant it, but a flag that, wherever it floats, is the symbol of freedom and equal rights for all. Democracy can never be extended by force, as you would fling a net over a flock of birds; but give it a chance and it will grow, as a tree grows, by sending down its roots into the heart of humanity and lifting its top toward the light and spreading its arms wider and wider until all the persecuted flocks of heaven find refuge beneath its protecting shade.

The ideal of American manhood, the ideal of American government, the ideal of American glory and influence—these three are the ancestral ideals that have been the strength and prosperity of America through the nineteenth century. Will they endure through the twentieth century?

Already we hear, in certain quarters, a prediction that they will be, at least in part, abandoned. More than this, there is even a demand, frankly voiced by some, that they should be cast aside in so far as they interfere with a new ideal of military and naval supremacy and the extension of territory by force of arms. This demand was clearly expressed by the Professor of History in Harvard University, writing in *Harper's Magazine* some six years ago. Speaking of the impossibility of applying the old ideals of government to the newly acquired territories, he says: "The only alternative is the rule of the few, and those few exercising power conferred by a distant administration. But that system means a change in American standards of government and human rights. We must give up our fine contempt for other nations which rule with

an iron hand; we must abandon the
principle that all just government depends on the consent of the governed;
we must look on the colonial status as
permanent and not a stage on the way
to Statehood; we must begin to settle
difficult questions of religion and worship by orders from Washington; we
must surround our colonial governors
with body-guards to arrest insurgent
leaders; we must either yield part of
our protective policy or give up the policy for which our forefathers fought
in the Revolution, that colonies exist for
their own benefit and not for the advantage of the mother country; we
must give up our principle of free in-
tercourse between the parts of our empire or else we must admit the Chinese
to the continent."

This is a plain statement, made by one
who approves the change which he pre-

dicts. I think it is true, though I doubt whether the American people have yet begun to realize its truth, or to weigh the price which must be paid in order that the United States may enter into an unembarrassed competition with these great nations whose motto is, "Conquer and Divide."

I am idealist enough to believe that when this realization comes; when under the pressure of circumstances which must ultimately, and at no distant time, arrive, we see more clearly the size and meaning of the sacrifice which is involved in giving up at least two of our inherited American ideals; then the third ideal—American manhood—will make its power felt to save and to restore the other two.

" Land that we love !   Thou future of the world !
Thou refuge of the noble heart oppressed !
Oh, never be thy shining image hurled
From its high place in the adoring breast

Of him who worships thee with jealous love !
Keep thou thy starry forehead as the dove
All white, and to the Eternal Dawn inclined !
Thou art not for thyself, but for mankind,
And to despair of thee were to despair
Of man, of man's high destiny, of God."

V

THE POWERS THAT BE

SAUL in Israel, Nebuchadnezzar in Babylon, Nero in Rome, William the Silent in Holland, Philip II. in Spain, George III. in Great Britain, Washington and Lincoln in America—all the powers that be, or have been, were ordained of God. And yet in every case the forces that have created them, and the causes that have exalted them, are to be sought in the character of the nations over which they have ruled. God ordains the power, but He ordains it to fit the people. A bandit-chief for a tribe of brigands, a tyrant for slaves, an inquisitor for bigots, a sovereign tax-collector for a nation of shop-keep-

ers, a liberator for a race of freemen.
The ruler is but the exponent of the
inmost thoughts, desires, and ambitions
of the ruled; sometimes their punishment, and sometimes their reward.

Therefore it may be said (subject to
those limitations and exceptions that are
always understood among intelligent
people when they speak in broad terms)
that as a general law, the people are
responsible for the character of their
rulers.

There are some complications which
obscure the operation of this law in a
monarchy, an empire, or an oligarchy.
A hereditary crown, a sword transformed into a sceptre, a transmitted
title, gives an opportunity to usurp or
extend unrighteous power. And yet
even here, a keen, clear eye can often
discern the people in the soveriegn. Napoleon raised his empire of conquest

cemented with blood, on a prepared
foundation in the heart of France filled
with the lust of military glory. George
III. obtained the power to nominate his
own ministers to carry out his policy of
colonial oppression, from a national conscience dulled by commercial rapacity
and a fat-witted spirit of contemptuous
indifference for the rights of others.

But in a republic the truth emerges
distinct and vivid, so that a child can
read it. The rulers are chosen from the
people by the people. The causes which
produce the men, and raise them to office, and clothe them with authority, are
in the heart of the people. Therefore in
the long run, the people must be judged
by, and answer for, the kind of men
who rule over them.

When we apply this law to the beginning of the history of the United States
it gives us ground for gratitude and

noble pride of birth. George Washington is the incarnation of the spirit of 1776, and the conclusive answer to all calumniators of the Revolution. No wild fanatic, no reckless socialist or anarchist, but a sober, sane, God-fearing, liberty-loving gentleman, who prized uprightness as the highest honour, and law as the bulwark of freedom, and peace as the greatest blessing, and was willing to live and die to defend them. He had his enemies who accused him of being an aristocrat, a conservative, a friend of the very England he was fighting, and who would have defamed and cast him down if they could. But the men of the Revolution held him up, because he was in their hearts, their hope and their ideal. God ordained him as a power, because the people chose him as their leader. And when we honour his memory, we honour theirs. "We praise famous men and our fathers that begat us."

But shall our children and our children's children have the same cause to thank and esteem us? Shall they say of us, as we say of our fathers, "They were true patriots, who loved their country with a loyal, steadfast love, and desired it to be ruled by the best men"?

That depends on one thing. Not on the chance of war, the necessity of revolution, the coming of a national crisis. The obligation of patriotism is perennial and its occasion comes with every year. In peace or war, in prosperity or in adversity, the true patriot is he who maintains the highest standard of honour, purity, and justice for his country's laws and rulers and actions. The true patriot is he who is as willing to sacrifice his time and strength and property to remove political shame and reform political corruption, as he would be ready to answer the call to battle against a foreign foe. The true patriot is he who works and votes, with the same courage that he would show in arms, in order that the aspirations of a noble people may be embodied in the noblest rulers. For, after all, when history completes the record and posterity pronounces the verdict, it is by the moral quality of their leaders and representatives that a people's patriotism must be judged.

It is true that the sharp crisis of war flashes light upon this judgment. In the crisis of liberty, Washington stands foremost as the proof that the Revolution was for justice, not for selfishness; for order, not for anarchy. In the crisis of equality, Lincoln stands foremost as the proof that the war for the Union was not a war of conquest over the South, but a war to deliver the captive and let the oppressed go free. Those two men were the central figures in the crises; but the causes which produced them, and supported them in the focus of light, while men of violence raged, and partisans imagined a vain thing, were hidden in the people's life and working in secret through years of peace and preparation.

And when the third crisis comes—the crisis of fraternity, in which it shall be determined whether a vast people of all sorts and conditions of men can live together in liberty and brotherhood, without standing armies or bloody revolts, without unjust laws which discriminate between the rich and the poor, and crush the vital force of individuality, and divide classes—in liberty and fraternity, with the least possible restraint and the greatest possible security of life and property and freedom of action—when

[110]

the imminent crisis comes in which this hope of our forefathers must be destroyed or fulfilled, the leaders who shall wreck or rescue it, and the ultimate results of that mighty conflict, will simply represent the moral character and ideals of the American people.

Now the causes which control the development of national character are threefold: domestic, political, and religious: the home, the state, and the church.

The home comes first because it is the seed-plot and nursery of virtue. A noble nation of ignoble households is impossible. Our greatest peril to-day is in the decline of domestic morality, discipline, and piety. The degradation of the poor by overcrowding in great tenements, and the enervation of the rich by seclusion in luxurious palaces, threaten the purity and vigour of old-fashioned

American family life. If it vanishes, nothing can take its place. Show me a home where the tone of life is selfish, disorderly, or trivial, jaundiced by avarice, frivolized by fashion, or poisoned by moral scepticism; where success is worshiped and righteousness ignored; where there are two consciences, one for private and one for public use; where the boys are permitted to believe that religion has nothing to do with citizenship and that their object must be to get as much as possible from the State and to do as little as possible for it; where the girls are suffered to think that because they have no votes they have therefore no duties to the commonwealth, and that the crowning glory of an American woman's life is to marry a foreigner with a title—show me such a home, and I will show you a breeding-place of enemies of the Republic.

To the hands of women the ordinance of nature has committed the trust of training men for their country's service. A great general like Napoleon may be produced in a military school. A great diplomatist like Metternich may be developed in a court. A great philosopher like Hegel may be evolved in a university. But a great man like Washington can come only from a pure and noble home. The greatness, indeed, parental love cannot bestow; but the manliness is often a mother's gift. Teach your sons to respect themselves without asserting themselves. Teach them to think sound and wholesome thoughts, free from prejudice and passion. Teach them to speak the truth, even about their own party, and to pay their debts in the same money in which they were contracted, and to prefer poverty to dishonour. Teach them to worship God by doing some useful work, to live honestly and cheerfully in such a station as they are fit to fill, and to love their country with an unselfish and uplifting love. Then they may not all be Washingtons, but they will be such men as will choose a Washington to be their ruler and leader in

"The path of duty and the way to glory."

And in the conflict between corporate capital and organized labour, if come it must, they will stand fast as the soldiers, not of labour nor of capital, but of that which is infinitely above them both—the commonwealth of law and order and freedom.

But the character of the people is not only moulded by the tone of domestic and social life, it is also expressed and influenced by the tone of political life, by the ideals and standards which prevail in the conduct of public affairs. And here, it must be confessed, our country discloses grave causes for anxiety. Our political standards have undoubtedly shifted from that foundation on which Washington placed them in his first inaugural, "the principles of private morality." Take, for example, the appearance of governors of sovereign States who excuse and defend the destruction of life and property which would be called murder and arson if it were the work of individuals, because it is committed by great labour-unions which control public sentiment and votes. Take for the great example the system of distributing public office as party spoils.

Without doubt, the Spoils System is an organized treason against the Republic and a transgression against the moral law. It is a gross and sordid iniquity. Its emblem should not be the eagle, but the pelican, because it has the largest pouch. It shamelessly defies three of the Ten Commandments. It lies, when it calls a public office a spoil. It covets, when it desires to control that office for the benefit of party. It steals, when it converts that office from the service of the commonwealth into a gift to "reward" a partisan, or a sacrifice to "placate" a faction.

It is an idle amusement for clever cynics in the newspapers, and amiable citizens in their clubs, to vituperate the Ring and the Boss, while they approve, sanction, or even tolerate the vicious principle, "To the victors belong the spoils." This principle is the root of the evils which afflict us. There can be no real cure except one which is radical. Police investigations and periodical attempts to "drive the rascals out" do not go deep enough. We must see and say and feel that the whole spoils system from top to bottom is a flagrant immorality and a fertile mother of vices. The Ring does not form itself out of the air; it is bred in the system. A Boss is simply a boil, an evidence of bad blood in the body politic. Let the bad blood out and he will subside.

Who are responsible for the civic corruption of some of the American States and cities? The corporations from whom the Boss gets his wealth in payment for his protection; the office-seekers, high or low, who go to the Boss for a place for themselves or for others; and the citizens who, by voting or not voting, have year after year filled our legislative chambers with men who were willing to do the bidding of the Boss for a consideration. If there is to be a radical and permanent cleansing, it can only be by

[117]

breaking up and eradicating the whole system of irresponsible and haphazard appointment to office, and by substituting for it the system of appointment for merit and fitness, under wise and just rules, which throw the civil service of nation, State, and city open, on equal terms, to every citizen who can prove that he is qualified to serve.

Think for a moment of what we have gained and what we have still to gain in this direction. There are 290,000 places in the Civil Service of the United States. Of these places, 154,000 have been classified under the rules. Since 1900, 59,000 have been added to the classified list. There are still 136,000 places which are outside of the classified service. It should be the desire and object of every patriotic American to remove these places as rapidly and as completely as possible from all chance of occupation or use by the spoils system. Burn the nests, and the rats will evacuate. Clean the sewers, and the malaria will abate.

But what have religion and the church to do with all these things? Just this: a free church in a free state should exercise a direct influence upon the moral tone of domestic and political life. If not, it is an impotent and useless parody on Christianity. The church is set as a light in the world. Do not let that light be put into a dark lantern and turned backward upon the Scribes and Pharisees. Set it on a candlestick that it may give light unto all that are in the house. Let the church shed the light of warning and reproof upon the immoral citizen who enjoys the benefits of citizenship and evades its responsibilities; the dishonest merchant who uses part of his gains to purchase political protection

[119]

and his good reputation to cover the transaction; the recreant preacher who denounces the corruptions of government "down in Judee" and ignores the same corruptions in the United States; the lawyers who study the laws in order to defend their clients in evading them; and the officials who profess to serve the state, and then add, "The state— that's *me*." But it is not only to expose and condemn the evil that the light of religion is needed. It should also shine to reveal and glorify the good. Let it fall upon the true heroes of the republic, the brave soldiers, the loyal citizens, the pure statesmen, that all men may know that the church recognizes these men as servants of the most high God because they are in deed and in truth the servants of the people.

It is to be remembered that the American church bore a noble part in the beginning of our national life, inspiring, purifying, and blessing the struggle for justice and liberty. It is not to be forgotten that she has a duty, no less sacred, in the conflicts of these latter days; to encourage men in the maintenance of that liberty which has been achieved and in the reform of all evils which threaten the purity of private and public life; to proclaim that our prosperity does not depend upon the false maxims of what are called "practical politics," but, as Washington said, upon "religion and morality, those great pillars of human happiness, those firmest props of the duties of men, and citizens."

With politics, so far as they have to do with the strife of parties and the rivalry of candidates, the church has no concern. But with *"polit-ethics"*— the moral aspect of the life of the state

—she must deal frankly and fearlessly. When she evades or neglects this office of public prophecy, when she gives her strength to theological subtlety and ecclesiastical rivalry and clerical millinery, and stands silent in the presence of corruption and indifferent to the progress of reform, her own bells will toll the death-knell of her influence, her sermons will be the funeral discourses of her power, and her music will be a processional to the grave of her lost honour. But when she proclaims to all people, without fear or favour, the necessity of a thorough-going conscience and a divine law of righteousness in every sphere of human life, the reverence of men will crown her walls with praise.

VI

THE FLOOD OF BOOKS

"THE world is cumbered with books," complained the wise man, two thousand years ago. "There are books here in Jerusalem and in Thebes and in Babylon and in Nineveh; even in Tyre and Sidon among the Philistines, no doubt one would find books. Still men go on scribbling down their thoughts and observations, in spite of the fact that there is nothing new under the sun. Where are the readers to come from, I wonder? For much study is a weariness of the flesh, and of making many books there is no end."

But what would the writer that was king say if he were alive to-day, when the annual output of books in this country alone is about five thousand, and when the printing-press multiplies these volumes into more than five million copies? Doubtless he would be much astonished, and perhaps even more displeased. But I conjecture that he would go on writing his own books, and that when they were done he would look for a publisher. For each age has its own thoughts and feelings; and each man who is born with the impulse of authorship thinks that he has something to say to his age; and even if it is nothing more than a criticism of other men for writing so much and so poorly, he wants to say it in his own language.

Thomas Carlyle, talking volubly on the virtues of silence, represents a *rôle* which is never left out in the drama of literature.

After all, is it not better that a hundred unnecessary books should be published than that one good and useful book should be lost? Nature's law of parsimony is arrived at by a process of expense. The needless volumes, like the infertile seeds, soon sink out of sight; and the books that have life in them are taken care of by the readers who are waiting somewhere to receive and cherish them.

Reading is a habit. Writing is a gift. Both may be cultivated. But I suppose there is this difference between them: the habit may be acquired by any who will; the gift can be developed only by those who have it in them to begin with. How to discover it and make the best of it, and use the writing gift so that it shall supply the real needs and promote the finest results of the reading habit,—that is the problem.

I do not know of any ready-made solution. The only way to work it out is for the writers to try to write as well as they can, and for the publishers to publish the best that they can get, and for the great company of readers to bring a healthy appetite, a clean taste, and a good digestion to the feast that is prepared for them. If anyone partakes not wisely but too much, that is his own fault.

No doubt a good many people are drawn to writing by slight and foolish motives, and they do their work foolishly and slightly. Every human occupation has a certain proportion of silly and superficial workers, to whom the work seems less important than the pay. But in the guild of letters there are also men and women of the better sort, to whom each year brings sincere delight in their work for its own sake.

Scholars have been sifting and arranging the results of their studies in great libraries. Observers of men and manners have been travelling and taking notes in strange lands and in the foreign parts of their own country. Teachers of life and morals have been trying to give their lessons a convincing and commanding form. Critics have been seeking to express the secrets of good work in arts and letters. Students of nature have been bringing together the records of their companionship with birds and beasts and flowers. Storytellers have been following their dream-people through all kinds of adventures to joyful or sorrowful ends. And poets, a few, have been weaving their most delicate fancies and their deepest thoughts into verse.

In what different places, and under what various conditions these men and women have been working! Some of

them in great cities, in rooms filled
with books; others in quiet country
places, in little "dens" of bare and
simple aspect; some among the tran-
quillizing influences of the mountains;
others where they could feel the inspiration of an outlook over the tossing, lim-
itless plains of the ocean; a few, perhaps, in tents among the trees, or in
boats on the sea,—though, for my part,
I find it difficult to understand how
anyone can actually write out-of-doors.
The attractions of nature are so close
and so compelling that it is impossible
to resist them. Out-of-doors for seeing
and hearing, thinking and feeling! In-
doors for writing!

It is pleasant to reflect upon the great
amelioration which has been made in
the "worldly lot" of writers, by the increase and wider distribution of the pecuniary rewards of authorship. It is not

necessary to go back to the age of Grub Street for comparison. There has been a change even since the days when Lowell wrote, "I cannot come [to New York] without any money, and leave my wife with 62½ cents, such being the budget brought in by my secretary of the treasury this week"; and when Hawthorne's friends had to make up a purse and send it to him anonymously, to relieve the penury caused by the loss of his position in the Custom-House at Salem. Nowadays, people who certainly do not write better than Lowell and Hawthorne, find life very much easier. They travel freely; they live in a comfortable house—some of them have two—with plenty of books and pictures. The man who would begrudge this improvement in the condition of literary workers must have, as Dr. Johnson would say, "a disposition

[129]

little to be envied." It is no more than
the world has done for the doctors and
the lawyers. Have not the profits of
book-making, on the material and commercial side, advanced even more rapidly? The wages of printers and paper-
makers and bookbinders are larger.
The fortunes of successful publishers
are increased. Why should not the
author have a share in the general
prosperity?

Besides, it should be remembered that
while there has been a certain enlarge-
ment in the pay of literary workers, it
has not yet resulted in opulence among
men of letters as a class. The principal
gain has been along the line of enlarged
opportunities and better remuneration
for magazine, newspaper, and editorial
work. Setting these aside, the number
of people who make a good living by
writing books is still very small. I will

not even attempt to guess how many there are; it might precipitate a long correspondence. But it is safe to say that there are not fivescore in America. What a slight burden is the support of a hundred authors among 80,000,000 people! Your share in the burden is a little more than one-millionth part of an author. What is that compared with the pleasure that you get out of new books, even though you are one of those severe people who profess to read none but old ones?

When I hear that the brilliant writer of "The Mountain of Derision" has just built a mansion at Laxedo, or that the author of "The Turning Point" is driving a four-in-hand through the White Mountains, it does not cause me a single pang of discontent. My contribution to that mansion, according to the present rate of royalty, was about forty cents, and to the support of the equipage I have given perhaps thirty cents. In each case I received good value for my money,—pleasant and, I trust, not unprofitable hours. This expense irks me far less than the extra two dollars a ton that I shall probably have to pay for coal this winter.

But I would not be understood as agreeing to the general proposition that the possession of four-in-hands and the like is necessary, or even favourable, to the production of good literature. Of course, if a man has extraordinary luck, he may find some competent person to take care of his luxuries for him, while he gives himself to the enjoyment of his work, and lives almost as comfortably as if he had never become rich. But, as a rule, it may be taken for granted that plain living is congenial to high thinking. A writer in one of the

[132]

English periodicals a couple of years ago put forth the theory that the increase of pessimism among authors was due to the eating of too much and too rich food. Among other illustrations he said that Ibsen was inordinately given to the pleasures of the table. However that may be, it is certain that the literary life, at its best, is one that demands a clear and steady mind, a free spirit, and great concentration of effort. The cares of a splendid establishment and the distractions of a complicated social life are not likely, in the majority of cases, to make it easier to do the best work. Most of the great books, I suppose, have been written in rather small rooms.

The spirit of happiness also seems to have a partiality for quiet and simple lodgings. "We have a little room in the third story (back)," wrote Lowell in

1845, just after his marriage, "with white curtains trimmed with evergreen, and are as happy as two mortals can be."

There is the highest authority for believing that a man's life, even though he be an author, consists not in the abundance of things that he possesses. Rather is its real value to be sought in the quality of the ideas and feelings that possess him, and in the effort to embody them in his work.

The work is the great thing. The delight of clear and steady thought, of free and vivid imagination, of pure and strong emotion; the fascination of searching for the right words, which sometimes come in shoals like herring, so that the net can hardly contain them, and at other times are more shy and fugacious than the wary trout which refuse to be lured from their hiding-places; the pleasure of putting the fit phrase in the proper place, of making a conception stand out plain and firm with no more and no less than is needed for its expression, of doing justice to an imaginary character so that it shall have its own life and significance in the world of fiction, of working a plot or an argument clean through to its inevitable close: these inward and unpurchasable joys are the best wages of the men and women who write.

What more will they get? Well, unless history forgets to repeat itself, their additional wages, their personal dividends under the profit-sharing system, so to speak, will be various. Some will probably get more than they deserve, others less.

The next best thing to the joy of work is the winning of gentle readers and friends who find some good in your book, and are grateful for it, and think kindly of you for writing it.

The next best thing to that is the recognition, on the part of people who know, that your work is well done, and of fine quality. That is called fame, or glory, and the writer who professes to care nothing for it is probably deceiving himself, or else his liver is out of order. Real reputation, even of a modest kind and of a brief duration, is a good thing; an author ought to be able to be happy without it, but happier with it.

The next best thing to that is a good return in money from the sale of a book. There is nothing dishonourable in writing for money. Samuel Johnson, in the days of his poverty, wrote *Rasselas* to pay the expenses of his mother's funeral.

But to take, by choice, a commercial

view of authorship, to write always with an eye on the market, to turn out copious and indifferent stuff because there is a ready sale for it, to be guided in production by the fashion of the day rather than by the impulse of the mind, —that is the sure way to lose the power of doing good work.

The best writing is done for its own sake. In the choice of a subject, in the manner of working it out, in the details of form and illustration, style, and diction, an author cannot be too jealous in guarding his own preference, ideal, inspiration,—call it what you will. Otherwise his book will lack the touch of personality, of independence, of distinction. It is here, perhaps, that a large part of the modern output of books fails to come up to the best standard.

But when a piece of work has been

done, freely, sincerely, thoroughly,—
done as well as the writer can do it,—
then it is safe. The new methods of pa-
per-making and printing and binding,
the modern system of publishing and
advertising, the admirable skill of the
artists who are now engaged in design-
ing illustrations and book-covers and
types, certainly cannot hurt the quality
of a book, and may do something to
help its sale. For this the honest author, having finished his work as nearly
as possible to his own satisfaction, and
disposed of it for the best price obtain-
able, should be duly grateful.

Amid the making of many books,
good literature is still produced, as it
was in the days of Thackeray and
Dickens, Carlyle and Ruskin, Tennyson and Browning, Irving and Hawthorne and Lowell and Emerson, out
of the hearts of men and women who

write because they love it, and who do
their work in their own way because
they know that, for them, it is the best
way.

VII

BOOKS, LITERATURE, AND THE PEOPLE

Lᴇᴛ us begin by trying to distinguish between the people and the public.

The public is that small portion of the people which is in the foreground at the moment. It is the mirror of passing fashions, the court of temporary judgments, the gramophone of new tunes.

The people is a broader, deeper word. It means that great and comparatively silent mass of men and women on which the public floats, as the foam floats on the wave. It means that community of human thought and feeling which lies behind the talk of the day.

There are many publics, for they change and pass. But the people are one.

In the realm of letters, as elsewhere, I hold to the principles of democracy. The people do not exist for the sake of literature: to give the author fame, the publisher wealth, and books a market. On the contrary, literature should exist for the sake of the people: to refresh the weary, to console the sad, to hearten up the dull and downcast, to increase man's interest in the world, his joy of living, and his sympathy with all sorts and conditions of men.

It is to be desired, no doubt, that the relation of American literature to the people should be made closer, deeper, and more potent, that it may not only express, but really enrich the common life, and so promote the liberty of the individual from the slavery of the su-

[141]

perficial, and wisely guide and forward the community in the pursuit of true happiness. But while we desire a further advance in this direction, it is well for us to remember that no advance is possible without a recognition of the ground already gained. Pessimism never gets anywhere. It is a poor wagon that sets out with creaking and groaning. Let us cheerfully acknowledge that the relations of literature to the people are probably better to-day than they have ever been before in the history of the world.

Freedom is a great gain. Open libraries are signs of progress.

Books are easier of access and possession, at the present time, than any other kind of food. They have become incredibly cheap, partly through the expiration of copyrights, and partly through the reduction in the cost of manufacture. I cannot think that the loss involved for certain classes in either of these processes is to be weighed for a moment against the resulting advantage to the people. The best books are the easiest to get, and, upon the whole, they have the widest circulation. Notably this is true of the most beautiful, powerful, and precious of all books— the English Bible, which is still the most popular book in the world.

Another good thing in which we must rejoice is the liberation of books from various kinds of oppression. The *Index Librorum Prohibitorum* still exists, but it is no longer what it used to be. The only officers of the Inquisition in the modern world of letters are the librarians; and, taken all in all, they exercise their power with mildness and beneficence.

The influence of party politics on the

fate of books is almost extinct. The days of literary partisanship, when the *Edinburgh Review* scalped the conservative writers, while the *Quarterly* flayed the liberals, are past.

The alleged tyranny of modern magazine editors is a gentle moral suasion compared with the despotism of the so-called patrons of art and letters in earlier times. Let anyone who thinks that there is too much literary log-rolling in the present day turn back to the fawning dedications of the Renaissance and the age of Queen Anne, and he will understand how far authorship has risen out of base subserviency into independence and self-respect.

Certainly the condition of the realm of letters is better, its relation to the people is closer, and its influence on the world is greater than ever before.

But this does not mean that there are

no evils to be removed, no dangers to be averted, and no further steps to be taken in advance.

Books are now sold in the dry-goods shops. No one can fairly object to that. But is there not some objection to dealing in books as if they were dry-goods?

A book can be bought for a nickel. There is no harm in that. But is there not considerable harm in advertising nickel-plated writing as sterling silver?

All that is necessary, at present, to sell an unlimited quantity of a new book is to sell the first hundred thousand, and notify the public. The rest will go by curiosity and imitation. Is there no danger in substituting popularity for perfection as the test of merit?

Five thousand books are published every year in England, and nearly as many more in America. It would be a selfish man who could find fault with an industry which gives employment and support to such a large number of his fellow men. But has there not come, with this plethora of production, an anæmia of criticism? That once rare disease, the *cacoëthes scribendi,* seems to have become endemic.

The public must like it, else it would not be so. But have the people no interests which will be imperilled if the landmarks of literary taste are lost in the sea of publication, and the art of literature is forgotten in the business of book-making?

Everyone knows what books are. But what is literature? It is the ark on the flood. It is the light on the candlestick. It is the flower among the leaves; the consummation of the plant's vitality, the crown of its beauty, and the treasure-house of its seeds. It is hard to define, easy to describe.

Literature is made up of those writings which translate the inner meanings of nature and life, in language of distinction and charm, touched with the personality of the author, into artistic forms of permanent interest. The best literature, then, is that which has the deepest significance, the most lucid style, the most vivid individuality, and the most enduring form.

On the last point contemporary judgment is but guesswork, but on the three other points it should not be impossible to form, nor improper to express, a definite opinion.

The qualities which make a book salable may easily be those which prevent it from belonging to literature. A man may make a very good living from his writings without being in any sense a man of letters. He has a perfect right to choose between the enrichment of the world by working along the line of his own highest ideal, and the increase of his bank account by running along the trolley-car track of the public fancy. He has the right to choose, but his choice places him.

On the other hand, the fact that a book does not sell is not in itself a sufficient proof that it is great. Poor books, as well as good ones, have often been unsuccessful at the start. The difference is that the poor ones remain unsuccessful at the finish. The writer who says that he would feel disgraced by a sale of fifty thousand copies cheers himself with a wine pressed from acid grapes, and very unwholesome. There is no reason why a book which appeals only to the author should be considered better than a book which appeals only to the public.

Neither is there any reason why a publisher of popular books should go to the opposite extreme and say that "there is no use under heaven for the critic; the man who buys the book is the real critic, and so discriminating is he that a publisher cannot sell a bad book." If this standard prevails, we shall soon hear the proud and happy publisher saying of a book in its hundredth thousand, as Gregory the Great is reported to have said of the Scripture, that "he would blush to have it subjected to the rules of grammar."

The true cause for blushing lies in the fact that criticism has been so much confused with advertisement; that so many of the journals which should be the teachers of the public have become its courtiers; that realism in its desire to be dramatic has so often turned to the theatre instead of to real life, and thus has become melodramatic; that virility (which is a good word in its place) has been so much overworked, and used as a cloak to cover a multitude of sins; and that the distinction between books and literature has been so often overlooked and so largely forgotten.

The public is content with the standard of salability. The prigs are content with the standard of preciosity. The people need and deserve a better standard. It should be a point of honour with men of letters to maintain it by word and deed.

Literature has its permanent marks. It is a connected growth, and its life-history is unbroken. Masterpieces have never been produced by men who have had no masters. Reverence for good work is the foundation of literary character. The refusal to praise bad work, or to imitate it, is an author's personal chastity.

Good work is the most honourable and lasting thing in the world. Four elements enter into good work in literature:

An original impulse—not necessarily a new idea, but a new sense of the value of an idea.

A first-hand study of the subject and the material.

A patient, joyful, unsparing labour for the perfection of form.

A human aim—to cheer, console, purify, or ennoble the life of the people. Without this aim literature has never sent an arrow close to the mark.

It is only by good work that men of letters can justify their right to a place in the world. The father of Thomas Carlyle was a stone-mason, whose walls stood true and needed no rebuilding. Carlyle's prayer was: "Let me write my books as he built his houses."

VIII

CHRISTIANITY AND CURRENT LITERATURE

In literature the inner life of man finds expression and lasting influence through written words. Races and nations have existed without it; but their life has been dumb and with their death their power has departed; they have vanished into thin air. What do we know of the thoughts and feelings of those unlettered tribes of white and black and yellow and red, flitting in ghost-like pantomime across the background of the world's stage? Whatever message of warning, of encouragement, of hope, of guidance they may have had for us remains undelivered.

They are but phantoms, mysterious and ineffective. But with the art of literature, life arrives at utterance and lasting power. The Scythian, the Etruscan, the Phœnician are dead. The Greek, the Hebrew, the Roman still live. We know them. They are as real and potent as the Englishman, the American, the German. They touch us and move us through a vital literature.

Religion is a life—the life of the human spirit in contact with the Divine. Therefore it needs a literature to express its meaning and perpetuate its power.

It is the fashion nowadays to speak scornfully of "a book religion." But where is the noble religion without a book? Men praise the "bookless Christ"; and the adjective serves as a left-handed criticism of his followers, who revere the Bible as their rule of faith and practice. True, he wrote no volume; but he absorbed one literature, the Old Testament; and he inspired another, the New Testament.

How wonderful, how supreme is the Bible as an utterance of life in literature! With what convincing candour are the hopes and fears, the joys and sorrows, the deep perplexities and clear visions of the heart of man under the divine process of education disclosed in its pages! What range! What history, biography, essays, epigrams, letters, poetry, fiction, drama—all are here. The thoughts breathe with inspiration, the figures live and move. And most of all, the central figure, Jesus Christ, long expected, suddenly revealed, seen but for a moment, imperishably remembered, trusted, and adored, stands out forever in the simple words of a few brief chapters, the clearest, most enduring, most potent personality in the world's history.

I do not hold with the saying that "the Bible is the religion of Protestants." If that were true, Protestants would be in the position of mistaking the expression for the life, the lamp for the light, the stream for the fountain. But I hold that without the Bible, Christianity would lose its vital touch with the past, and much of its power upon the present. It would be like a plant torn from its roots and floating in the sea.

Christianity owes an immense part of its influence in the world to-day to the place of the Bible in current literature. What other volume is current in a sense so large and splendid? What book is so widely known, so often quoted, so deeply reverenced, so closely read by learned and simple, rich and poor, old and young? Wherever it comes it enriches and ennobles human life, opens common sources of consolation and cheer, helps men to understand and respect one another, gives a loftier tone to philosophy, a deeper meaning to history, and a purer light to poetry. Strange indeed is the theory of education that would exclude this book, which Huxley and Arnold called the most potent in the world for moral inspiration, from the modern school-house. Stranger still the theory of religion which would make of this book a manual of ecclesiastical propagandism rather than the master-volume of current literature.

"Beware of the man of one book," says the proverb. The saying has two meanings. The one-book man may be strong, and therefore masterful; he may also be narrow, and therefore dangerous. The Bible exercises its mightiest and most beneficent influence, not when it is substituted for all other books, but when it pervades all literature.

Christianity needs not only a sacred Scripture for guidance, warning, instruction, inspiration, but also a continuous literature to express its life from age to age, to embody the ever-new experiences of religion in forms of beauty and power, to illuminate and interpret the problems of existence in the light of faith and hope and love.

Close this outlet of expression, cut off this avenue of communication, and you bring Christianity into a state of stagnation and congestion. Its processes of thought become hard, formal, mechanical; its feelings morbid, spasmodic, hysterical; its temper at once oversensitive, and dictatorial. It grows suspicious of science, contemptuous of art, and alienated from all those broader human sympathies through which alone it can reach the outer world. Insulated, opinionated, petrified by self-complacency, it sits in a closed room, putting together the pieces of its puzzle-map of doctrine, and talking to itself in a theological dialect instead of speaking to the world in a universal language.

Books it may produce—books a-plenty! Big fat books of dogmatic exposition; little thin books of sentimental devotion; collections of sermons in innumerable volumes; pious puppet-show story-books in which the truth or falsehood of certain dogmas is illustrated by neatly labelled figures stuffed with sawdust and strung on wires. And these an insulated Christianity, scornful of what it calls mere literary art and unsanctified charm, would persuade us to accept as a proper religious library. But John Foster spoke the truth in his essay, "On Some of the Causes by which Evangel-

ical Religion has been Rendered Un-
acceptable to Persons of Cultivated
Taste," when he calls these books "a
vast exhibition of the most subordinate
materials that can be called thought, in
language too grovelling to be called
style." Certainly they are not literature,
nor is it either to be wondered at or
much regretted that they are not current. They do not propagate religion;
they bury it.

Very different are the works by which
the vital spirit of Christianity has been
expressed, the vivifying influence of
Christianity extended in the world of
modern thought and feeling. There
are sermons among them, like the
discourses of South and Barrow and
Liddon and Bushnell; and religious
meditations like the *Confessions of
St. Augustine* and *The Imitation of
Christ;* and books of sacred reasoning

[159]

like the *Provincial Letters* of Pascal, and Butler's *Analogy of Natural and Revealed Religion;* and divine epics and lyrics like those of Dante and Milton and George Herbert and Cowper and Keble.

But there are also books which are secular in form, neither claiming nor recognizing ecclesiastical sanction, presenting life in its broad human interest, and at the same time inevitably revealing the ethical, the spiritual, the immortal as the chief factors in the divine drama of man.

Christian literature includes the best of those writings in which men have interpreted life and nature from a Christian stand-point. The stand-point does not need to be always defined or described. A man who looks from a mountain-peak tells you not of the mountain on which he stands, but of

what he sees from it. It is not necessary
to name God in order to revere and
obey him. I find the same truth to life
in *King Lear* as in the drama of Job:
and the same sublime, patient faith,
though the one ends happily and the
other sadly. *The Book of Ruth* is no
more and no less Christian, to my mind,
than Tennyson's *Dora*. There is the
same religion in *The Heart of Mid-
lothian* as in *The Book of Esther*. The
parable of the rich man lives again
in *Romola*. In *Dr. Jekyll and Mr.
Hyde* St. Paul's text, "The flesh lust-
eth against the spirit," is burned deep
into the memory.

No great writer represents the whole
of Christianity in its application to
life. But I think that almost every
great writer, since the religion of Jesus
touched the leading races, has helped
to reveal some new aspect of its beau-

ty, to make clear some new secret of its sweet reasonableness, or to enforce some new lesson of its power. I read in Shakespeare the majesty of the moral law, in Victor Hugo the sacredness of childhood, in Goethe the glory of renunciation, in Wordsworth the joy of humility, in Tennyson the triumph of immortal love, in Browning the courage of faith, in Thackeray the ugliness of hypocrisy and the beauty of forgiveness, in George Eliot the supremacy of duty, in Dickens the divinity of kindness, and in Ruskin the dignity of service. Irving teaches me the lesson of simple-hearted cheerfulness, Hawthorne shows me the intense reality of the inner life and the hatefulness of sin, Longfellow gives me the soft music of tranquil hope and earnest endeavour, Lowell makes me feel that we must give ourselves to our fellow men if we would bless them, and Whittier sings to me of human brotherhood and divine fatherhood. Are not these Christian lessons?

I do not ask my novelist to define and discuss his doctrinal position, or to tell me what religious denomination he belongs to. I ask him to tell me a story of life as it is, seen from the point of view of one who has caught from Christianity a conception of life as it ought to be. I do not ask him even to deal out poetic justice to all his characters, and shut the prison-doors on the bad people while he rings the wedding-bells for the good. I ask him only to show me good as good and evil as evil; to quicken my love for those who do their best, and deepen my scorn for those who do their worst; to give me a warmer sympathy with all sorts and conditions of men who are sincere and loyal and kind; to strengthen my faith that life is worth living even while he helps me to realize how hard it is to live; to leave me my optimism, but not to leave it stone-blind; not to depress me with cheap cynicism, nor to lull me with spurious sentimentalism, but to nourish and confirm my heart in Sir Walter Scott's manly faith, that "to every duty performed there is attached an inward satisfaction which deepens with the difficulty of the task and is its best reward."

The use of fiction either to defend or to attack some definite theological dogma seems to me illegitimate and absurd. I remember a devout and earnest brother who begged me to write a story to prove that Presbyterians never held the doctrine of infant damnation. I would as soon write a story to prove that Bacon wrote Shakespeare's plays.

But that fiction may serve a noble

purpose in renewing our attraction to virtue, in sharpening our abhorrence of selfishness and falsehood, in adding to the good report of the things that are pure and lovely, in showing that heroism is something better than "eccentricity tinged with vice," and, at its deepest, in making us feel anew our own need of a divine forgiveness for our faults, and a divine Master to control our lives—that is true, beyond a doubt; for precisely that is what our best fiction from *Waverley* down to *The Bonnie Brier Bush* and *Sentimental Tommy* has been doing. Name half a dozen of the great English novels at random — *Henry Esmond, David Copperfield, The Cloister and the Hearth, Lorna Doone, Romola, The Scarlet Letter*—and who shall dare to deny that there is in these books an atmosphere which breathes of the vital

[165]

truths and the brightest ideals of Christianity?

It must be admitted that there are many books, current at present, of which this cannot be said. Some of them breathe of patchouli and musk, some of stale beer and cigarettes, some of the gutter and the pest-house, many do not breathe at all. But I do not see in this any great or pressing danger. The chemists tell us that the paper on which these books are printed will not last twenty years. It will not need to last so long, for the vast majority of the books will be forgotten before their leaves disintegrate. Superficial, feeble, fatuous, inane, they pass into oblivion; and the literature which abides is that which recognizes the moral conflict as the supreme interest of life, and the message of Christianity as the only real promise of victory.

There are three mischievous and perilous tendencies in our modern world against which the spirit of Christianity, embodied in a sane and manly and lovable literature, can do much to guard us.

The first is the growing idolatry of military glory and conquest. It is one thing to admit that there are certain causes for which a Christian may lawfully take the sword, it is another thing to claim, as some do, that war in itself is better for a nation than peace, and to look chiefly to mighty armaments on land and sea as the great instruments for the spread of civilization and Christianity. The forerunner of Christ was not Samson, but John the Baptist. The kingdom of heaven cometh not with observation, nor with acquisition, nor with subjugation. If all the territory of the globe were subject to one conquering emperor to-day, no matter though the cross were blazoned on his banner and his throne, the kingdom of heaven would not be one whit nearer. "Not by might, nor by power, but by my spirit, saith the Lord." That is the message of Christianity. A literature that is Christian must exalt love, not only as the greatest, but as the strongest thing in the world. It must hold fast the truth bravely spoken by one of America's foremost soldiers, General Sherman, that "war is hell." It must check and reprove the lust of conquest and the confidence of brute force. It must firmly vindicate and commend righteousness and fair-dealing and kindness, and the simple proclamation of the truth, as the means by which alone a better age can be brought nigh and all the tribes of earth taught to dwell together in peace. It must repeat Wordsworth's fine message:

" By the soul
Only the nations shall be great and free."

The second perilous tendency is the growing idolatry of wealth. Money is condensed power. But it is condensed in a form which renders it frightfully apt to canker and corrupt. A noble literature, truly in harmony with the spirit of Christ, will expose, with splendid scorn and ridicule, the falsehood of the standard by which the world, and too often the church, measure what a man is worth by his wealth. It will praise and glorify simple manhood and womanhood. It will teach that true success is the triumph of character, and that true riches are of the heart.

The third perilous tendency is the growing spirit of frivolity. A brilliant British essayist in writing a life of Robert Browning lately took occasion to remark that the nineteenth century had already become incomprehensible to us because it took life so seriously. This was probably not intended as a compliment; but if the nineteenth century could hear the criticism it would have good reason to feel flattered. An age that does not take life seriously will get little out of it. One of the greatest services that Christianity can render to current literature is to inspire it with a nobler ambition and lift it to a higher level.

I remember an old woodsman in the Adirondack forest who used to say that he wanted to go to the top of a certain mountain as often as possible, because it gave him such a feeling of "heaven-up-histedness." That is an uncouth, humble, eloquent phrase to describe the function of a great literature.

"Unless above himself he can
    Erect himself, how mean a thing is man!"

[170]

I want the books that help me out of the vacancy and despair of a frivolous mind, out of the tangle and confusion of a society that is buried in *bric-à-brac,* out of the meanness of unfeeling mockery and the heaviness of incessant mirth, into a loftier and serener region, where, through the clear air of serious thoughts, I can learn to look soberly and bravely upon the mingled misery and splendour of human existence, and then go down with a cheerful courage to play a man's part in the life which Christ has forever ennobled by his divine presence.

IX

THE CHURCH IN THE CITY

THE very things that make the church most needed in the city are the things that make it hard for the church to survive there. The throng and pressure of multitudinous life, the intensity of business competition and social emulation, the extravagance of wealth and the exigencies of poverty, the scarcity of time and the superabundance of pastime, the presence of crowds and the absence of fellowship, the avarice-chill and the amusement-fever, the vitality of vice and the nervous prostration of virtue, the rush and whirl and glare and busy emptiness of a life at top speed—

in these things the church finds its opportunity, its call, and its danger.

If the city church is to fill its place, and do its proper work, and survive, it must have two things: first, a clear idea of the mission to which Christ has appointed it; second, a firm purpose to fulfil that mission and not to die while there is work to do.

The church in the city is not to be conformed to the fashion of the surrounding world. It is a great mistake to suppose that men and women want from the city church what they can get, and do get, anywhere else in the city— glitter and bustle and display and rivalry and superficial entertainment. They want something very different; and that something is religion; and religion means inward purity and peace and joy, the sense of God's nearness, the comfort of Christ's love, the strength that comes from spiritual food and fellowship.

It may seem inconsistent to say this after what I have already said of the city. But the truth generally resides in apparent contradictions. The characteristics of city life intensify the necessity of religion. The peril of the city church lies in the temptation to make itself an annex and an imitation, rather than a refuge and a contrast. The church must always be separate from the world, in the sense that the church has something distinct and different to offer. Not a Sunday lecture-hall, a sacred concert-room, an ecclesiastical millinery-shop, a baptized social club, or a disguised money-making corporation—none of these things does the city need from the church, but "a house of prayer for all nations"; a place where divine truth seems clearer, and human brotherhood dearer, and heaven a little nearer, than anywhere else in the roaring town.

Separate from the world the church must be; but never shut off from the world. Not blind to the facts of city life, not insensible to its necessities, not indifferent to its peculiar and pressing problems, but wide-awake to all these things, close to the business and bosoms of the men and women for whose service it exists. The church must move forward with the tide of modern progress, keeping abreast of the development of the city in order that it may meet the city's need. The model described in the book of Genesis is a good model for a Noah's ark. But Noah has been dead for some time. The church is not an ark, but a life-boat. In building a life-boat you will do well to follow the most modern lines and use the latest equipment. The aim of the church is not to keep on doing the same thing forever in the same way, but to improve the way as often as may be necessary to keep on accomplishing the same thing.

The problem of denominationalism meets the city church. On this corner is a house of worship that is called Presbyterian, on the next one that is called Episcopalian, on the next one that is called Baptist or Methodist, and so on. What does this mean but that good people have different tastes and predilections in matters of form and formula? It does not mean that they are enemies. Let each church be true to its own type, and recognize that the city has room and need for all types. And if the types become less crude, less angular, less extreme, by virtue of friendly contact; if each learns something from the others, that also is natural and profitable. I should be ashamed if I could not worship gladly in any church where Christ is confessed as Lord; and I should be sorry if I had not some memories which make the church of my father and mother a little sweeter, a little more home-like, than any other. What the city demands of all the different kinds of churches is loyalty to type, liberty of growth, and largeness of heart and mind in common service.

The problem of institutionalism meets the city church. My personal conviction on that question can be put into a sentence. The church may well have a soup-kitchen, if it is needed; but the church ought never to be a soup-kitchen. That kind of beneficence which ministers to bodily need and has no word for the soul, that kind of social service which is carefully devitalized from all spir-

itual purpose, belongs, if anywhere, to
the state, not to the church. When the
church gives a cup of cold water to a
little child, it must be done in the Master's name. When the church ministers
to the sick, the afflicted, the imprisoned,
it must seek in them what the Master
sought—their souls, to save them from
sin. Bread? Yes, let the church deal
bread to the hungry, but never fail to
give a blessing with the bread.

The problem of success meets the city
church. Its work is costly, its situation
is trying, its necessities are immediate.
A city church will not run long on the
momentum of the past, nor survive
many years on the strength of a reputation. It must succeed or die. Yes, but
what does it mean for the church to
succeed? Only this: to win the affection,
confidence, support, and loyalty of the
people, by doing its own work and ful-

filling its own mission. The church can succeed only by deepening, strengthening, purifying, the influence of religion in the city. Success on any other basis —fashionable, financial, sensational— means, for the church at least, a living death.

True, you sometimes see a city church which is distinctly separate from the world, rigidly opposed to its fashions, very strict in discipline, and very orthodox in doctrine, slowly shrivelling up and dying out. Why? Because it has refrained from being conformed to the fashion of the world? No! But because it has forgotten to be transformed by the renewing of its mind. Because it has kept the righteousness of the kingdom, and left out the peace and the joy in the Holy Ghost. Because its long prayers and strict rules and correct doctrines have become dry, dull, and

[179]

mechanical. It has lost the note of spiritual gladness and power. It is losing its hold on the city, not because it is too religious, but because it is not quite religious enough to rejoice in God, and let its joy shine through. The right kind of a church for the city is one which, however simple its worship, however small its congregation, is manifestly filled with the spirit of consolation, love, and good cheer. Everyone who enters it feels at once, "These people are glad to be Christians, and glad to have me with them, and truly it is good to be here." Such a church will survive, and in the best sense of the word succeed.

Somewhere I have read or heard a German story of a certain poor man who always used to go about his work in such a spirit of joy and contentment, with such beautiful visions shining in his eyes, that he was called "the dreamer." When he married, his home seemed to be full of the same ideal peace and gladness. His wife and children were visited by the same visions. When a friend asked how it came to pass, the man confessed that he carried around with him all the time the dream that he was a king, and that his wife was the queen, and that the boys and girls were princes and princesses. They all shared the dream, and they lived it out pleasantly together, so that every pleasure was a royal entertainment and every meal was a royal feast. Thus their common life was lifted up and beautified.

The dream of the poor man is the reality of religion. The message of the Gospel is that men and women are all sons and daughters of God. The church that brings this message and makes us feel its truth, amid the noise and turmoil

[181]

and weariness and oppression of city life, is the right kind of a church for the city. It delivers us from bondage. It shows us how to be happy. It helps us to be good.

X

PROPERTY AND THEFT

THE relation of Christianity to communism has become a question for thoughtful people to consider seriously, if they wish to preserve their intellectual candour and self-respect in adhering to the religion of Jesus. The reason for this is curious and interesting.

The communists of the earlier type were for the most part sturdy, and sometimes violent, opponents of Christianity, and indeed of all religions, except such as they themselves occasionally invented. With this kind of communism, men who sincerely professed to hold the Christian faith had, of course, no question of relation to consider. It was already settled that it must be war.

But in recent times a new type of communism has arisen, which has laid aside the red cap and put on the white cravat. It discusses the problem of the organization of society on ethical and religious grounds. 'The real social unit,' says modern communism, 'is not the individual, but the community, and a person is only a fraction, who can have no right to possess anything which the community needs or wants. The law which pretends to confer such a right upon an individual — the law which says, for example, that under certain conditions you may become the rightful owner of a piece of land, which you may use, or sell, or leave to your heirs, and which shall not be taken from you without due compensation— such law is essentially immoral and irreligious, because it protects and rewards a form of selfishness. All things really belong to all men; and the man who wishes to gain a title to any portion of the earth, however small, is in effect willing to rob his fellow-men of that which God has given to them all in common. The idea of private property has something fundamentally unrighteous about it. The teachings of the Bible are against it. The spirit of Jesus, who was really a great socialist, is altogether in favour of common ownership. If those who profess to follow him were truly in sympathy with his doctrine and willing to apply it to everyday life, they would confess that what we now call property is only another form of theft, and would do their best, at all hazards, to abolish an institution so selfish, unjust, and unchristian.'

Thus modern communism, at least in

one of its manifestations, instead of professing hostility to Christianity, claims alliance with it, and justifies itself by an appeal to the moral and religious authority of the Bible. Not very long ago a candidate for the mayoralty of New York City (an honourable man, and one who polled sixty-seven thousand votes) affirmed that every man who owned his home was practically a robber of the community, and supported the accusation by quoting the Old Testament. A preacher, of wide fame and influence, declared from the pulpit that the early Christian church at Jerusalem was distinctly communistic, and that this is "the animus of the New Testament." Assertions like these, which are not exceptional, but are frequently made by men of undoubted sincerity and probity and benevolence, are certainly not to be ignored by in-

[186]

telligent Christians who value their own spiritual integrity.

If property is theft, according to the teachings of Jesus, then the church itself, like the temple of old, has become a den of thieves. If the animus of the New Testament is distinctly communistic, then every honest Christian is bound either to give up his faith in the holy scripture or to obey its doctrine not only in the letter, but in the spirit, and to work with those who are seeking to establish a new order of society in which private possessions shall be unknown.

No man can get any comfort or strength out of his religion if he suspects himself of disloyalty to it in his daily transactions.

The sense of the terrible inequalities of human life under present conditions, the increased knowledge of the privations and sufferings of the poor, the misery that is condensed in great cities, the hardship that embitters toil in lonely and desolate regions, the dim consciousness of the manifold want and woe that men and women and little children are enduring in this tangled world, press heavily upon sensitive spirits in these days. If all this wretchedness were the fruit of a false social order, contrary to the law of God and the spirit of Christ; if the Bible revealed a remedy for it all in the doctrine of communism, which Christians were too ignorant or selfish or cowardly to accept or apply, then it would be no wonder that the people who play traitor to their own religion should find that it no longer brings them inward peace and joy. They would deserve to be ill at ease, anxious, full of fears and forebodings. They would deserve to be of all men most miserable.

But suppose that, after all, it should be true that human poverty and want and wretchedness do not spring from any single fault in the social order, but from a deeper source: the selfish and wilful evil that dwells in the heart of man. Suppose that the remedy which Christianity reveals should turn out to be something very different from communism: not the abolition of private property, but the use and control of it by the spirit of fair play and wise love. Then the church, still feeling the pressure of human misery upon her heart, and confessing her want of greater wisdom and larger love in seeking to lighten the burdens of men, could yet face her problem with courage and a steady mind. She need have no sense of fatal inconsistency in declining the alliance which communism claims. She could try to follow the spirit of Christ more faithfully, without surrendering her leadership to the men who demand a social revolution.

This is the situation, then, which the new type of communism forces us to face. Those who are sincere in accepting Christianity as the true religion, and the Bible as its rule of faith and practice, must meet the question fairly and consider it seriously. Was Jesus a communist at heart? Are the laws which enable men to own their homes, and to save money for their children, an offence to him? What does the Bible really teach about property and theft?

Two cases are quoted from the Bible to prove that it has at least a partial leaning toward the communistic theory.

The first is the Hebrew Year of Jubilee, which is used as an argument for the nationalization of land.

Now, when we study the Old Testament carefully we find that there is not a word of historic record to show that the Year of Jubilee ever went into practical operation; nor is there a single passage to indicate that this peculiar institution, given to a peculiar people under peculiar circumstances, was ever intended to be an example for all nations at all times. To claim that it was, would be as unreasonable as to argue that the Jewish method of slaughtering animals should be imposed on all butchers.

But waiving these objections, and looking at the Year of Jubilee as a possible model for legislation in our times, we see that it was simply an iron-clad law of entail, more rigid than England has ever known. It provided that the land should always remain in the families among whom it had been divided at the conquest of Canaan. It could neither be alienated by an individual, nor confiscated by the state. If a man was forced to sell his land by stress of poverty, the utmost that he could dispose of was a title to the usufruct for as much of the fifty years as might remain before the next Jubilee. At any time he might redeem it; and at the end of the fixed period every man inevitably "returned unto his possession."

Suppose a company of Irish immigrants arriving in Judea under the operation of this law: they could have bought city property, for that was specially exempt from its provisions; they could have rented farms from the native aristocracy; but not one of those Hibernians, nor one of their children, nor one of their grandchildren, could ever have acquired a share in one square inch of the soil of the country. Any man who admires this system is at liberty to say so; but it is hardly probable that anyone will try to put it into practice, nor does it look much like what we commonly understand by the nationalization of land, which is to make the earth as free as the air and the light to all men.

The second case which is quoted from the Bible in favour of communism is the example of the early church at Jerusalem. It is described in the second and fourth chapters of the Book of Acts. The characteristic feature of it is, that the believers in Christ "were together and had all things common; and sold their possessions and goods, and parted them to all, as every man had need."

But surely this does not imply a denial of the rights of private property. For if an individual could not really own

anything, how could there be any buy-
ing or selling? If the fact of birth
gives everyone an equal claim upon all
the good things of the world, how could
these Christians, a mere handful in the
city, defend their funds against the
Jews and the heathen? What right had
they to confine their benefactions, as
they did, to their fellow-believers, instead of sharing all things with their
brother-men? It would be an unfortunate thing for the widows and or-
phans of our great cities if the modern
churches should adopt the strict plan
of the Jerusalem Christians. For, in
point of fact, their experiment was
simply the exercise of the right of
every man to do as he chooses with his
own; and they chose to live together
and help each other. It was a fraternal
stock company for mutual aid and protection. No man was bound to come into

it unless he wished; but if he did come in, he was bound to act honestly.

Read what St. Peter said to that hypocrite, Ananias, about his land: "While it remained, was it not thine own? And after it was sold, was it not in thine own power?" It would be difficult to imagine a stronger statement of the rights of property under the most trying circumstances. Of course it is possible for any band of men who like the Jerusalem system to re-establish it today; but its result of pauperism in the primitive church was not particularly encouraging, nor would it bring us one step nearer to the communistic ideal of general ownership and distribution by the state.

There are some other cases which are not frequently quoted by modern communists, but which have a direct bearing upon the doctrine of the Bible in regard to the rights of private property. There is the case of Naboth and his vineyard.

Naboth was a landholder. He had inherited a field from his ancestors. It belonged to him, and therefore no one else had a right to build on it or to cultivate it. The vines which he had planted there were his own. He could eat the grapes, or make wine out of them, or give them to the village children. The "unearned increment" which had come to that field from the building of the royal palace in the neighborhood was a part of Naboth's property. He could do with it as he liked—keep it, or rent it, or sell it.

Ahab was a king. He represented the state. He was the anointed of the Lord, and he wanted that vineyard. He had not the nerve to take it by violence, nor the cleverness to squeeze Naboth out with a tax. So he tried to buy it, and failing, took to his bed and turned his face to the wall. But Queen Jezebel was a woman of larger resources. She contrived a plan to get rid of Naboth; and then she invited her husband to go down and enjoy the confiscated property. And as he stood in the vineyard, trembling with uncertain pleasure, that man of iron, Elijah the prophet, found him, and cursed him in the name of the just God, promising that his race should perish in shame because of the evil that he had done.

It was not merely because Ahab had connived at the death of a man. Many a king of Israel had done worse without incurring a special revelation of divine wrath. But Ahab had violated a sacred right of property. He had trampled upon a principle of justice which made that poor man's vineyard his own, to have and to hold against all comers, whether they were greedy kings or envious beggars. There is not the slightest hint that Naboth was wronging anybody in owning that land; but there is the plainest teaching that in trying to take it away from him against his will the King was a thief; and for that, God promised that he should die among the dogs, that he should perish as a landless vagabond.

It must be admitted that the Old Testament holds out scanty encouragement to the advocates of communism. But perhaps we shall find something in the New Testament to support the notion that private property is unjust and ought to be speedily abolished.

What shall we say then of Jason of Thessalonica, and Lydia of Philippi, and Titus Justus of Corinth, and Philip of Cæsarea, who all received the apostles into their own houses? Were these people engaged in perpetuating a cruel and oppressive distinction between the rich and the poor?

Turn to the gospels. There was a man in Bethany named Lazarus, who had a house in which he sheltered the Christ whom the community had rejected. There was a man named Zaccheus, who was rich and who entertained Jesus at his own house. Is there any suggestion that the Master disapproved of these property owners? There was a man named Joseph of Arimathea, who had a garden and a new sepulchre in which he made a quiet resting-place for the body of him whom the people had despised and crucified. Was he a selfish robber?

Christianity never would have found a foothold in the world, it never would have survived the storms of early persecution, had it not been sheltered in its infancy by the rights of private property, which are founded in justice, and therefore are respected by all lovers of righteousness, Christian or heathen. It is difficult to see how the religion of Jesus could have sanctioned these rights more emphatically than by using them for its own most holy purposes.

But someone may say that this is only the lower side of Christianity; that there is a higher side which enforces charity and unselfish benevolence and universal brotherhood; and that in the development of these things the lower side is destined to disappear, and communism will become the order of society. Truly, it would be difficult to exaggerate the emphasis which is laid not only by Christ and His apostles, but also by the Old Testament writers, upon the duties of kindness and generosity and compassion for the needy. But these teachings are perfectly consistent with those other instructions of the Bible which enjoin diligence in business, and fidelity to contracts, and respect for the property of others.

The Bible teaches that God owns the world. He distributes to every man according to his own good pleasure, conformably to general laws. Under the operation of these laws a man may acquire such a title to certain things that for any other man, or community of men, to attempt to dispossess him without full compensation is robbery. Nor is there any difference in this respect between the property of the rich and the property of the poor. If it be fairly acquired by honest industry, lawful inheritance, or just exchange, the one is as sacred as the other. I read to-day that the savings-banks of New York State held $1,250,000,000 of deposits. Most of this money has been laid up by people who work for wages. And if the bulk of this capital should go, as it probably will, into the purchase of homes for families, the law of God still declares that it must neither be stolen nor confiscated, nor even coveted, by private robber or public thief.

There is a fundamental and absolute difference between the doctrine of the Bible and the doctrine of communism. The Bible tells me that I must deal my bread to the hungry; communism tells the hungry that he may take it for himself. The Bible teaches that it is a sin to covet; communism says that it is the new virtue which is to regenerate society. Communism maintains that every man who is born has a right to live; but the Bible says that if a man will not work neither shall he eat; and without eating, life is difficult. Communism

[202]

holds up equality of condition as the ideal of Christianity; but Christ never mentions it. He tells us that we shall have the poor always with us, and charges us never to forget, despise, or neglect them. Christianity requires two things from every man that believes in it: first, to acquire his property by just and righteous means; and, second, to "look not only on his own things, but also on the things of others."

This condemns the reckless greed of the gold-worshippers, and the cruelty of conscienceless corporations, and the dishonesty of law-dodging sharpers; but it condemns equally the communistic theories which propose to sweep away or disregard the rights of private ownership. When the communist says that the public lands which are still held by the state ought to be retained, or distributed according to a new system,

he is simply propounding an economic
theory which may or may not be sound.
But when he says that the real estate
which has become private property
ought to be practically confiscated, by
taxation or in any other way, he is simply teaching us to call theft by a longer
name. It is not a question of expedi-
ency; it is a question of righteousness.

I have entire confidence in the sincere
philanthropy and generous motives of
many of the men who have been drawn
into a partial approval of communistic
doctrines. I have a profound sympathy
with them in hatred of all tyranny and
oppression, in hearty desire for the
amelioration of society and the relief of
all unnecessary suffering. Surely that
is at least one of the objects of Christianity, to improve the present condition of humanity, to make the whole
world not only better, but also happier.

If there are any men and women who live in fat contentment with their own physical comfort, and shut their ears to the cry of the distressed, they are not true disciples of the compassionate Jesus, and the Bible promises that they shall have a heavy reckoning at the day of judgment.

But it does not seem likely that the evils of society can be cured by moving along the line of communism. History warns us that every experiment in that direction has been a failure. Free corn filled Rome with hungry idlers. The communistic poor laws of 1815 made England howl with want and shame and crime. There is no reason to suppose that men in the mass are any more wise or kind or benevolent than they are as individuals. The idea of an all-absorbing, all-controlling, all-disbursing state is a Frankenstein monster.

Even to coquet with it in theory is to increase the miseries of society.

It is in the interest of no separate class, but of all mankind, that we hold fast to the old-fashioned doctrine of the rights of property coupled with the duties of charity. The asylums and hospitals of New York City now draw the greater part of their support from the Christian benevolence of between three and four thousand persons. What will become of those institutions if the springs which feed them are destroyed? Does anyone think that the Board of Aldermen, or the Labour Party, or the city at large would do the work better?

The advocates of communism, in their revision of the Bible, would give us an improved version of the parable of the Good Samaritan. They would tell us that when the proud Levite and the selfish Priest had passed by the wounded

man, a kind communist came down that
way and began to whisper in the suf-
ferer's ear: "My friend, you have been
much in error. You were a thief yourself when you were amassing your private wealth; and these gentlemen who
have just relieved you of it with needless violence have only begun, in a hasty
and unjustifiable manner, what must
soon be done, in a large and calm way,
for the benefit of the whole community." Whereupon, we are to suppose,
the man was much enlightened and
comforted, and would have become a
useful member of society,—if he had
lived.

But Christ says that it was a Samaritan, a man of property, riding on his
own beast and carrying a little spare
capital in his pocket, who lifted up the
wounded stranger, and gave him oil and
wine, and brought him into a place of

security, and paid for his support. And to everyone who hears the parable Christ says: "Go thou and do likewise." Here is the open secret of the regeneration of society in the form of a picture.

If we want it in the form of a philosophy, we may get it from St. Paul in five words:

"Let him that stole, steal no more"— that is *reformation;* "but rather let him labour"—that is *industry;* "working with his hands that which is good"— that is *honesty;* "that he may have" —that is *property;* "to give to him that needeth"—that is *charity.*

XI

THE CREATIVE IDEAL OF
EDUCATION

In that admirable book, *The American Commonwealth*, by Mr. James Bryce, the chapter on colleges and universities comes immediately after the chapter on Wall Street. There is a singular contrast between them: for, while the one represents the nearest approach to pessimism in an uncommonly cheerful book, the other marks the highest note of optimism to which a British writer can allow his impressions to rise. The Wall Street chapter closes with the melancholy remark that the habits of speculation, constitutional excitability, and high nervous tension seem to have passed into the fibre of the American people. But the chapter on colleges and universities ends with the hopeful observation that, "while of all the institutions of the country they are those of which the Americans speak most modestly, and indeed deprecatingly, they are those which seem to be at this moment making the swiftest progress, and which have the brightest promise for the future."

In regard to the habit of modest and deprecating speech, we have a faint suspicion that the author's experience of academic anniversaries may have been limited. Perhaps he was here in the dull season. Perhaps he went only to Boston or Chicago.

But in regard to the recognition of our educational growth as one of the brightest and most promising features of the American commonwealth, there can be no doubt that it is an accurate observation and a wise judgment. No other expansion of the republic can be compared, in magnitude or in meaning, with the expansion of education. No other assurance of protection against those perils of American life which are popularly symbolized by Wall Street, can be compared with the fact that democratic communities have recognized the wisdom and the necessity of building up those safeguards of national sanity, integrity, and liberty which are typified, in their highest development, by the university.

It is to education that we look for protection against the spirit of

"Raw haste, half-sister to delay "—

against the blind and reckless temper of gambling—against the stupid idolatry of mere riches, either in the form of servile flattery or in the disguise of equally servile envy. Education must give us better standards of success and higher tests of greatness than gold can measure. Education must clarify public opinion, calm and allay popular excitability, tranquillize and steady American energy, dispel local and sectional prejudice, and strengthen the ties which bind together all parts of our common country.

Now, these are great expectations. We cannot hope to have them realized, even in part, unless we give to our whole educational effort, which is really bound together from the primary school up to the university, the highest aim, the true direction, the right movement. What, then, is the true ideal of education in a great democracy like the United States?

It is not a sufficient answer to this question to observe that since education is derived from the Latin *e-duco*, its true purpose must be the bringing out of what is in man. This definition is simple, but not satisfactory. There are many things in man, and there are various methods of bringing them out. The question is, What are the best things, and which is the best method of development?

There is, for example, a method of bringing out the grain of wood by a combination of stain and varnish. It is a superficial way of enhancing the natural difference between pine and poplar and black walnut. Sometimes it is used as a device for disguising the difference between cherry and mahogany. Is this a true type of education?

There is also a method of bringing

out the resources of the earth by working it for the largest immediate returns in the market. Farms are exhausted by overcropping; pastures desolated by overstocking; mines worked out for a record yield. Fictitious values are evolved and disposed of at transitory prices. Much that is marketable is brought out in this way. Is this a true type of education?

There is also a method of bringing out the possibilities of a living plant by culture, giving it the needed soil and nourishment, defending it from its natural enemies, strengthening its vitality and developing its best qualities. This method has been used, in the experiments of Mr. Luther Burbank, in a way that seems almost miraculous, changing the bitter to the sweet, the useless to the useful, and proving that by a progressive regeneration one may

[214]

hope in time to gather grapes of thorns and figs of thistles. Is this a true type of education?

These three illustrations of different methods of "bringing things out" represent in picture the three main educational ideals which men have followed. Back of our various academic schemes and theories, back of the propositions which are made by college presidents for the adoption of new methods or the revival of old methods, back of the fluent criticisms which are passed upon our common schools and universities, lies the question of the dominant aim in teaching and learning. What should be the ideal of education in a democracy—the decorative ideal, the marketable ideal, or the creative ideal?

I speak of the decorative ideal first, because, strangely enough, it is likely to take precedence in order of time, and certainly it is pre-eminent in worthlessness. Barbarous races prefer ornament to decency or comfort in dress. Alexander von Humboldt observed that the South American Indians would endure the greatest hardships in the matter of insufficient clothing rather than go without the luxury of brilliant paint to decorate their naked bodies. Herbert Spencer used this as an illustration of the preference of the ornamental to the useful in education.

The decorative conception of education seems to be the acquisition of some knowledge or accomplishment which is singular. The impulse which produces it is not so much a craving for that which is really fine, as a repulsion from that which is supposed to be common. It is a desire to have something in the way of intellectual or social adornment which shall take the place of a mantle of peacock's feathers or a particularly rich and massive nose-ring.

This ideal not only rejects, contemns, and abhors the useful, but it exhibits its abhorrence by exalting, commending, and cherishing the useless, chiefly because it is less likely to be common. It lays the emphasis upon those things which have little or no relation to practical life. It speaks a language of its own which the people cannot understand. It pursues accomplishments whose chief virtue is that they are comparatively rare, and puts particular stress upon knowledge which is supposed to bestow a kind of gilding or enamel upon the mind. This ideal is apt to be especially potent in the beginning of a democracy, and to produce a crop of "young ladies' finishing schools" and "young gentlemen's polishing academies" singularly out of proportion to the real needs of the country. In its later development it brings forth all kinds of educational curiosities and abortions.

In this second crop of the decorative school of culture we find those strange phenomena of intellectual life which are known under the names of Æstheticism and Symbolism and Decadentism and the like. Their mark is eccentricity. Their aim is the visible separation of the cultured person from the common herd. His favourite poet must be one who is caviar to the vulgar. His chosen philosopher must be able to express himself with such obscurity that few, if any, can comprehend him. He must know more than anyone else about the things that are not worth knowing, and care very passionately for the things that are not usually considered worth caring about. He must believe that

Homer and Dante and Milton and the Bible have been very much overrated, and carefully guard himself, as Oscar Wilde did in the presence of the ocean, from giving way to sentiments of vulgar admiration. His views of history must be based upon the principle of depreciating familiar heroes and whitewashing extraordinary villains. He must measure the worth of literature by its unpopularity, and find his chief joy in the consciousness that his tastes, his opinions, and his aspirations are unlike those of common people.

But the favourite sphere of decorative culture is the realm of art. For here it finds the way to distinction easiest and most open. The degradation and torpor, the spirit of ignorance and blind perversity which fell upon the arts of design and expression in the middle of the last century, and which still prevail to a considerable extent among those whom Matthew Arnold used to revile as the Philistines of England and America, made it necessary to begin a reform. Certain artists who were very much in earnest (call them pre-Raphaelites, or men of the new renaissance, or Impressionists, or musicians of the future, or what you will) took up the work, and won, together with a great deal of ridicule, a large reward of fame. In their wake has followed the motley throng of æsthetes, great and small, learned and unlearned, male and female and neuter; the people who talk about art because they think it is fine; who discover unutterable sentiments in beds and tables, stools and candlesticks; who go into raptures over a crooked-necked Madonna after they have looked into their catalogues and discovered that it was painted by Botticelli; and

[220]

who insist with ecstatic perversity that the worst of Wagner is better than the best of Beethoven. It is the veriest simian mimicry of artistic enthusiasm, a thing laughable to gods and men.

True art—large, generous, sincere— "the expression of noble emotions for right causes"—is a noble and ennobling study. But art as a fashion, with its cant, its affectation, its blind following of the blind, is a poor inanity. There is no use for it in a democracy—nor indeed anywhere in this world which was created by the Great Lover of Truth and Hater of Shams. The intellectual *poseur*, the shallow and self-satisfied æsthete is the last person who is entitled to set up a claim to the possession of the true theory and the ripe result of education.

At the opposite extreme from the decorative ideal lies the marketable ideal of education. Its object, broadly stated, is simply to bring out a man's natural abilities in such a way that he shall be able to get the largest return in money for his work in the practical affairs of life. Nothing is of value, according to this ideal, which is not of direct utility in a business or a profession. Nothing counts which has not an immediate cash value in the world's market.

"Send my boy to high-school and college!" says the keen man of business. "What good will that do him? Seven years at the dead languages and higher mathematics will not teach him to make a sharp bargain or run a big enterprise." He thinks he has summed up the whole argument. But he has only begged the question. The very point at issue is whether the boy is a tool, to be ground and sharpened for practical use, or a living creature, whose highest value is to be realized by personal development.

The influence of this cash-value theory of culture may be seen in many directions.

It shows itself in certain features of our common-school system, not in the places where it is at its best, but in the places where it is controlled by politicians, sectarians, or cranks. It is far too mechanical. The children are run through a mill. They are crammed with rules and definitions, while their ideas and feelings are left to take care of themselves. Their imagination, that most potent factor of life, is entrusted to the guidance of the weekly story-paper, and their moral nature to the guidance of chance. The overworked and underpaid teacher is forced, by a false system of competition, to pack their little minds as full as possible of rules which they do not understand, and definitions which do not define, and assorted fragments of historical, geographical, chemical, mechanical, and physiological knowledge, which are supposed to have a probable market value.

It would be a good thing if the cities and towns of America would spend twice as much as they are spending to-day for common-school education. It would be a good thing if we could have twice as many teachers, and twice as intelligent, especially for the primary grades. And then it would be a good thing if we could sweep away half the "branches" that are now taught, and abolish two-thirds of the formal examinations, and make an end of competitions and prizes, and come down, or rather come up, to the plain work of teaching children to read intelligently

and write clearly and cipher accurately
—the foundation of a solid education.

The marketable ideal of culture makes
itself felt, also, to a considerable extent,
in some of the higher institutions of
learning. We can trace its effects in the
tendency to push the humanities aside,
and to train the young idea, from the
earliest possible period, upon the trellis
of a particular trade. Every branch,
every tendril which does not conform to
these lines must be cut off. The impor-
tance of studies is to be measured by
their direct effect upon professional
and industrial success. The plan is to
educate boys, not for living, but for
making a living. They are to be cultivated not as men, but as journalists,
surveyors, chemists, lawyers, physicians,
manufacturers, mining engineers, sell-
ers of wet and dry goods, bankers, ac-
countants, and what not.

In obedience to this theory, the attention of the student is directed from the outset to those things for which he can see an immediate use in his chosen pursuit. Literature is spoken of in academic circles as a mere embellishment of the solid course; and philosophy is left to those odd fellows who are going into the ministry or into teaching. The library is no longer regarded as a spiritual palace where the student may live with the master-minds of all the ages. It has taken on the aspect of a dispensary where useful information can be procured in small doses for practical purposes. Half-endowed technical schools spring up all over the land, like mushrooms after a shower. We have institutes of everything, from stenography to farriery; it remains only to add a few more, such as an Academy of Mesmerism, a College of Mind

Healing, and a Chiropodists' University, to round out the encyclopædia of complete culture according to the commercial ideal.

Let no one imagine that I mean to say a word against trade schools. On the contrary, I would speak most heartily in their support. So far as they do their work well they are an admirable and needful substitute for the earlier systems of apprenticeship for the various trades. Democracy needs them. They are really worth all the money that is put into them. But the error lies in supposing that they can take the place of the broader and higher education. By their own confession they move on another level. They mean business. But business is precisely the one thing which education does not mean. It may, doubtless it will, result in making a man able to do his own special work

[227]

in a better spirit and with a finer skill.
But this result is secondary, and not
primary. It is accomplished by forgetting the specialty and exalting the
man.

True education must begin and continue with a fine disregard of pecuniary
returns. It must be catholic, genial, dis-
interested. Its object is to make the
shoemaker go beyond his last—"*Sutor
ultra crepidam*"—and the clerk beyond
his desk, and the surveyor beyond his
chain, and the lawyer beyond his brief,
and the doctor beyond his prescription,
and the preacher beyond his sermon.

Special training, with an eye fixed on
some practical pursuit, works directly
the other way, and against the interests
of a true democracy. It deepens the
lines which separate men. It divides
them into isolated trades which become
close corporations, and into rival guilds

which defend themselves by blocking all avenues of intercommunication.

But the right culture for a democracy is that which opens the avenues of mutual comprehension, and increases the common ground of humanity. It broadens and harmonizes men on the basis of that which belongs to all mankind. If it elevates certain persons above their fellows, it does not therefore separate them from the race, but joins them to it more broadly. It lifts them as the peaks of a mountain-range are lifted, with a force that spreads the base while it raises the summit. The peaks are the unifying centres of the system. And the springs that rise among the loftiest hills flow down joyfully through the valleys and the plains.

The right ideal of education in a democracy is the creative ideal. It does not seek to adorn men with certain rare accomplishments which shall be the marks of a Brahminical caste. It does not seek to train men for certain practical pursuits with an eye single to their own advantage. It seeks, by a vital culture, to create new men, and new kinds of men, who shall be of ever-increasing worth to the republic and to mankind.

Creation, as it is now interpreted, is a process of development. If this interpretation be true, the result is none the less creative. Species originate, whether their origin be swift or slow.

Education is the human analogue of creation. Its beginning is the unfolding of something which already exists. But its aim, its motive, its triumphant result, is the production of something which did not exist before.

The educated man is a new man. It is not merely that he knows more. It is not merely that he can do more. There is something in him which was not there when his education began. And this something gives him a new relation to the past, of which it is the fruit, and to the future, of which it is the promise. It is of the nature of an original force which draws its energy from a new contact with the world and with mankind, and which distributes its power throughout life in all its channels.

This, it seems to me, is the real object and the right result of education; to create out of the raw stuff that is hidden in the boy a finer, stronger, broader, nobler type of man.

In using this language I am not dealing in glittering generalities. The better manhood of which I speak as the aim of education is no vague and nebulous thing—the dim delight of sensational preachers and virile novelists. It

has four definite marks: the power to
see clearly, the power to imagine vividly, the power to think independently,
and the power to will nobly. These are
the objects that the creative ideal sets
before us, and in so doing it gives us
a standard for all educational effort,
from the kindergarten to the university; a measure of what is valuable in
old systems and of what is desirable
in new theories; and a test of true success in teaching and learning.

I care not whether a man is called
a tutor, an instructor, or a full professor; nor whether any academic degrees adorn his name; nor how many
facts or symbols of facts he has stored
away in his brain. If he has these four
powers—clear sight, quick imagination,
sound reason, and right, strong will—I
call him an educated man and fit to be
a teacher.

I use the word "sight" to denote all those senses which are the natural inlets of knowledge. Most men are born with five, but comparatively few learn the use of even one. The majority of people are like the idols described by the psalmist: "Eyes have they, but they see not: they have ears, but they hear not: noses have they, but they smell not." They walk through the world like blind men at a panorama, and find it very dull. There is a story of an English-woman who once said to the great painter Turner, by way of comment on one of his pictures: "I never saw anything like that in nature." "Madam," said he, "what would you give if you could?"

The power to use the senses to their full capacity, clearly, sensitively, pene-tratingly, does not come by nature. It is the fruit of an attentive habit of

veracious perception. Such a habit is
the result of instruction applied to the
opening of blind eyes and the unseal-
ing of deaf ears. The academic studies
which have most influence in this direction are those which deal principally
with objective facts, such as nature-
study, language, numbers, drawing,
and music.

But the education of perceptive power
is not, and cannot be, carried on exclu-
sively in the study and the class-room.
Every meadow and every woodland is
a college, and every city square is full
of teachers. Do you know how the
stream flows, how the kingfisher poises
above it, how the trout swims in it, how
the ferns uncurl along its banks? Do
you know how the human body bal-
ances itself, and along what lines and
curves it moves in walking, in running,
in dancing, and in what living charac-

ters the thoughts and feelings are written on the human face? Do you know the structural aspect of man's temples and palaces and bridges, of nature's mountains and trees and flowers? Do you know the tones and accents of human speech, the songs of birds, the voices of the forests and the sea? If not, you need creative culture to make you a sensitive possessor of the beauty of the world.

Every true university should make room in its scheme for life out-of-doors. There is much to be said for John Milton's plan of a school whose pupils should go together each year on long horseback journeys and sailing cruises in order to see the world. Walter Bagehot said of Shakespeare that he could not walk down a street without knowing what was in it. John Burroughs has a college on a little farm beside the

Hudson; and John Muir has a university called Yosemite. If such men cross a field or a thicket they see more than the seven wonders of the world. That is culture. And without it, all scholastic learning is arid, and all the academic degrees known to man are but china oranges hung on a dry tree.

But beyond the world of outward perception there is another world of inward vision, and the key to it is imagination. To see things as they are—that is a precious gift. To see things as they were in their beginning, or as they will be in their ending, or as they ought to be in their perfecting; to make the absent, present; to rebuild the past out of a fragment of carven stone; to foresee the future harvest in the grain of wheat in the sower's hand; to visualize the face of the invisible, and enter into the lives of all sorts and conditions of

unknown men—that is a far more precious gift.

Imagination is more than a pleasant
fountain; it is a fertilizing stream.
Nothing great has ever been discovered
or invented without the aid of imagination. It is the medium of all human
sympathy. No man can feel with another unless he can imagine himself in
the other man's place.

The chief instrument in the education
of imagination is literature. The object
of literary culture is very simple. It is
to teach a man to distinguish the best
books, and to enable him to read them
with inward vision. The man who has
read one great book in that way has become a new creature and entered a new
world. But in how many schools and
colleges does that ideal prevail? We are
spending infinite toil and money to produce spellers and parsers and scanners.

We are trying hard to increase the number of people who can write with ease, while the race of people who can read with imagination is left to the care of chance. I wish that we might reverse the process. If our education would but create a race of readers, earnest, intelligent, capable of true imaginative effort, then the old writers would not be forgotten, and the new ones would get a wiser welcome when they arrive.

But the design of education is not accomplished unless a man passes beyond the power of seeing things as they are, and beyond the power of interpreting and appreciating the thoughts of other men, into the power of thinking for himself. To be able to ask, "Why?" and to discover what it means to say, "Because"—that is the intellectual triumph of education.

"To know the best that has been

thought and said in the world," is what Matthew Arnold calls culture. It is an excellent attainment. But there is a step beyond it, that leads from culture into manhood. That step is taken when the student, knowing something of the best that other men have thought and said, begins to think his own thoughts clearly through and to put them into his own words. Then he passes through instruction into education. Then he becomes a real person in the intellectual world.

The mere pursuit of knowledge is not necessarily an emancipating thing. There is a kind of reading which is as passive as massage. There is a kind of study which fattens the mind for examination like a prize pig for a county fair. No doubt the beginning of instruction must lie chiefly in exercises of perception and memory. But at a certain point the reason and the judgment must be awakened and brought into voluntary play. As a teacher I would far rather have a pupil give an incorrect answer in a way which showed that he had really been thinking about the subject, than a literally correct answer in a way which showed that he had merely swallowed what I had told him, and regurgitated it on the examination paper.

It seems to me, then, that a teacher should give his pupils rules in such a form that they can use them to work out their own problems. He should instruct them in languages so that words may serve to express clearly and accurately their own thoughts. He should teach them science in order that they may form habits of accurate observation, careful induction, and moderate statement of laws which are not yet fully understood. And if his instruction goes on to philosophy, history, literature, jurisprudence, government, his aim should be to give his pupils some standards by which they can estimate the works and ways, the promises and proposals of men to-day. Pupils thus educated will come out into the world prepared to take a real part in its life. They will be able to form an opinion without waiting for an editorial in their favourite newspaper. They will not need to borrow another man's spectacles before they can trust their eyes.

"My mind to me a kingdom is,"

wrote the quaint old courtly poet, Sir Edward Dyer. But how many there are, in all classes of society, who have no right to use his words. Discrowned monarchs, exiled and landless, desolate and impotent, wearied with trivial cares and dull amusements, enslaved to mas-

[241]

ters whom they despise and tasks which promise much and pay little—what possession is there that they can call their own, what moment of time in which they are not at the beck and call of other men, either grinding stolidly at their round in the treadmill or dancing idiotically to the uncomprehended music of some stranger's pipe? We often say of one whom we wish to blame slightly and to half excuse, "He is only thoughtless." But there is no deeper word of censure and reproach in human speech, for it signifies one who has renounced a rightful dominion and despised a kingly diadem.

The great dream of education as a loyalist of the democracy is that "the king shall have his own again"—that no prince or princess of the blood royal of humanity shall be self-exiled in the desert of thoughtlessness or chained in the slavery of ignorance. A lofty dream, a distant dream, it may be, but the only way toward its fulfilment lies through the awakening of the reason. Not to leave the people in a dull servitude of groping instincts, while the chosen few look down on them from the cold heights of philosophy; but to diffuse through all the ranks of society an ever-increasing light of quiet, steady thought on the meaning and the laws of life—that is the democratic ideal. Slowly or swiftly we may work toward it, but only along that line will the people win their heritage and keep it: the power of self-rule, through self-knowledge, for the good of all.

But one more factor is included in the creative ideal of education, and that is its effect upon the will. The power to see clearly, to imagine vividly, to think independently, will certainly be wasted, will be shut up in the individual and kept for his own selfish delight, unless the power to will nobly comes to call the man into action and gives him, with all his education, to the service of the world.

An educated man is helpless until he is emancipated. An emancipated man is aimless until he is consecrated. Consecration is simply concentration, plus a sense of duty.

The final result of true education is not a selfish scholar, nor a scornful critic of the universe, but an intelligent and faithful citizen who is determined to put all his powers at the service of his country and mankind.

What part are our colleges and universities to play in the realizing of this ideal of creative education? Their true function is not exclusive, but inclusive. They are to hold this standard of manhood steadily before them, and recognize its supreme and universal value wherever it is found.

Some of the most thoughtful men in the country have not been college-bred. The university that assumes to look down on these men is false to its own ideal. It should honour them, and learn from them whatever they have to teach. College education is not to be separated from the educative work which pervades the whole social organism. What we need at present is not new colleges with a power of conferring degrees, but more power in the existing colleges to make men. To this end let them have a richer endowment, a fuller equipment, but, above all, a revival of the creative ideal. And let everything be done to bring together the high school, the normal school, the grammar school, the primary school, and the little-red-schoolhouse school, in the harmony of this ideal. The university shall still stand in the place of honour, if you will, but only because it bears the clearest and most steadfast witness that the end of education is to create men who can see clearly, imagine vividly, think steadily, and will nobly.

XII

THE SCHOOL OF LIFE

MANY fine things have been said
in commencement addresses about
"Culture and Progress," "The Higher
Learning," "American Scholarship,"
"The University Spirit," "The Woman's College," and other subjects bearing on the relation of education to life.
But the most important thing, after
all,—the thing which needs not only to
be said, but also to be understood,—is
that life itself is the great school.

This whole framework of things visible and invisible wherein we mysteri-
ously find ourselves perceiving, reasoning, reflecting, desiring, choosing, and

acting, is designed and fitted, so far at least as it concerns us and reveals itself to us, to be a place of training and enlightenment for the human race through the unfolding and development of human persons such as you and me.

For no other purpose are these wondrous potencies of perception and emotion, thought and will, housed within walls of flesh and shut in by doors of sense, but that we may learn to set them free and lead them out. For no other purpose are we beset with attractions and repulsions, obstacles and allurements, tasks, duties, pleasures, persons, books, machines, plants, animals, houses, forests, storm and sunshine, water fresh and salt, fire wild and tame, a various earth, a mutable heaven, and an intricate humanity, but that we may be instructed in the nature of things and people, and rise by knowledge and sympathy, through gradual and secret promotions, into a fuller and finer life.

Facts are teachers. Experiences are lessons. Friends are guides. Work is a master. Love is an interpreter. Teaching itself is a method of learning. Joy carries a divining rod and discovers fountains. Sorrow is an astronomer and shows us the stars.

What I have lived I really know, and what I really know I partly own; and so, begirt with what I know and what I own, I move through my curriculum, elective and required, gaining nothing but what I learn, at once instructed and examined by every duty and every pleasure.

It is a mistake to say, "To-day education ends, to-morrow life begins." The process is continuous: the idea into the purpose, the purpose into the action, the action into the character. When the mulberry seed falls into the ground and germinates, it begins to be transformed into silk.

This view of life as a process of education was held by the Greeks and the Hebrews—the two races in whose deep hearts the stream of modern progress takes its rise, the two great races whose energy of spirit and strength of self-restraint have kept the world from sinking into the dream-lit torpor of the mystic East, or whirling into the blind, restless activity of the barbarian West.

What is it but the idea of the school of life that sings through the words of the Hebrew psalmist? "I will instruct thee and teach thee in the way which thou shalt go. I will guide thee with mine eye. Be ye not as the horse or as the mule, whose mouth must be held in with bit and bridle lest they come near unto thee." This warning against the mulish attitude which turns life into a process of punishment, this praise of the eye-method which is the triumph of teaching—these are the notes of a wonderful and world-wide school.

It is the same view of life that shines through Plato's noble words: "This then must be our notion of the just man, that even when he is in poverty or sickness, or any other seeming misfortune, all things will in the end work together for good to him in life and death; for the gods have a care of anyone whose desire is to become just, and to be like God, as far as man can attain his likeness by the pursuit of virtue."

Not always, indeed, did the Greek use so strong an ethical emphasis. For him the dominant idea was the unfolding of reason, the clarifying of the powers of thought and imagination. His ideal

[251]

man was one who saw things as they are, and understood their nature, and felt beauty, and followed truth.

It was the Hebrew who laid the heavier stress upon the conception of righteousness. The foundations of his school were the tablets on which the divine laws, "Thou shalt" and "Thou shalt not," were inscribed. The ideal of his education was the power to distinguish between good and evil, and the will to choose the good, and the strength to stand by it. Life, to his apprehension, fulfilled its purpose in the development of a man who walked uprightly and kept the commandments.

Thus these two master-races of antiquity, alike in their apprehension of existence from the standpoint of the soul, worked out their thought of vital education, along the lines of different temperaments, to noble results. Æschylus and Ezekiel lived in the same century.

Reason and Righteousness: what more can the process of life do to justify itself than to unfold these two splendid flowers on the tree of our humanity? What third idea is there that the third great race, the Anglo-Saxon, may conceive, and cherish, and bring to blossom and fruition?

There is only one—the idea of Service. Too much the sweet reasonableness of the Greek ideal tended to foster an intellectual isolation; too much the strenuous righteousness of the Hebrew ideal gave shelter to the microbe of Pharisaism. It was left for the Anglo-Saxon race, quickened by the new word and the new life of a divine Teacher, to claim for the seed an equal glory with the flower and the fruit; to perceive that righteousness is not reasonable, and reason is not righteous, unless they are both communicable and serviceable; to say that the highest result of our human experience is to bring forth better men and women, able and willing to give of that which makes them better to the world in which they live.

This is the ultimate word concerning the school of life. I catch its inspiring note in the question of that very noble gentleman, Sir Philip Sidney, who said: "To what purpose should our thoughts be directed to various kinds of knowledge, unless room be afforded for putting it into practice, so that public advantage may be the result?" These then are what the education of life is to bring out—Reason, Righteousness, and Service.

But if life itself be the school, what becomes of our colleges and universi-

[254]

ties? They are, or they ought to be, simply preparatory institutions to fit us to go on with our education. Not what do they teach, but how do they prepare us to learn—that is the question. I measure a college not by the height of its towers, nor by the length of its examination papers, nor by the pride of its professors, but chiefly by the docility of its graduates. I do not ask, Where did you leave off? but, Are you ready to go on? Graduation is not a stepping out; it is either a stepping up—*gradu ad gradum*—a promotion to a higher class, or a dropping to a lower one. The cause for which a student is dropped may be invincible ignorance, incurable frivolity, or obstructive and constrictive learning.

"One of the benefits of a college education," says Emerson, "is to show a boy its little avail." Hamilton and Jef-

ferson and Madison and Adams and
Webster were college men. But Frank-
lin, Washington, Marshall, Clay, and
Lincoln were not.

A college education is good for those
who can digest it. The academic atmosphere has its dangers, of which the
greatest are a certain illusion of infalli-
bility, a certain fever of intellectual
jealousy, and a certain dry idolatry of
schedules and programmes. But these
infirmities hardly touch the mass of
students, busy as they are nowadays
with their athletics, their societies, their
youthful pleasures. The few who are
affected more seriously are usually
cured by contact with the larger world.
Most of the chronic cases occur among
those who really never leave the preparatory institution, but pass from the
class to the instructor's seat, and from
that to the professorial chair, and so

along the spiral, bounded ever by the same curve and steadily narrowing inward.

Specialists we must have; and to-day we are told that a successful specialist must give his whole life to the study of the viscosity of electricity, or the value of the participial infinitive, or some such pin-point of concentration. For this a secluded and cloistered life may be necessary. But let us have room also in our colleges for teachers who have been out in the world, and touched life on different sides, and taken part in various labours, and been buffeted, and learned how other men live, and what troubles them, and what they need. Great is the specialist, and precious; but I think we still have a use for masters of the old type, who knew many things, and were broadened by experience, and had the power of vital inspiration, and could start their pupils on and up through the struggles and triumphs of a lifelong education.

There is much discussion nowadays of the subjects which may be, or must be, taught in a college. A part, at least, of the controversy is futile. For the main problem is not one of subjects, but of aim and method. "Liberal studies," says Professor S. H. Butcher, one of the finest living teachers of Greek, "pursued in an illiberal spirit, fall below the mechanical arts in dignity and worth." There are two ways of teaching any subject: one opens the mind, the other closes it.

The mastery of the way to do things is the accomplishment that counts for future work. I like the teacher who shows me not merely where he stands, but how he got there, and who encourages and equips me to find my own path through the maze of books and the tangled thickets of human opinion.

Let us keep our colleges and universities true to their function, which is preparatory and not final. Let us not ask of them a yearly output of "finished scholars." The very phrase has a mortuary sound, like an epitaph. He who can learn no more has not really learned anything. What we want is not finished scholars, but well-equipped learners; minds that can give and take; intellects not cast in a mould, but masters of a method; people who are ready to go forward wisely toward a larger wisdom.

The chief benefit that a good student may get in a good college is not a definite amount of Greek and Latin, mathematics and chemistry, botany and zoölogy, history and logic, though this in itself is good. But far better is the power to apprehend and distinguish, to weigh evidence and interpret facts, to think clearly, to infer carefully, to imagine vividly. Best of all is a sense of the unity of knowledge, a reverence for the naked truth, a perception of the variety of beauty, a feeling of the significance of literature, and a wider sympathy with the upward-striving, dimly groping, perplexed and dauntless life of man.

I will not ask whether such a result of college training has any commercial value, whether it enables one to command a larger wage in the marketplace, whether it opens the door to wealth, or fame, or social distinction; nor even whether it increases the chance of winning a place in the red book of *Who's Who*. These questions are treasonable to the very idea of education, which aims not at a marketable product, but at a vital development. The one thing certain and important is that those who are wisely and liberally disciplined and enlightened in any college enter the school of life with an advantage. They are "well prepared," as we say. They are fitted to go on with their education in reason and righteousness and service under the great Master.

I do not hold with the modern epigram that "the true university is a library." Through the vast wilderness of books flows the slender stream of literature, and often there is need of guidance to find and follow it. Only a genius or an angel can safely be turned loose in a library to wander at will. Nothing is more offensive than the complacent illusion of omniscience begotten in an ignorant person by the haphazard reading of a few volumes of philosophy or science.

There is a certain kind of reading that is little better than an idle habit, a substitute for thought. Of many books it may be said that they are nothing but the echoes of echoing echoes. If a good book be as Milton said, "the precious life-blood of a master-spirit, embalmed and treasured," still the sacred relic, as in the phial of St. Januarius at Naples, remains solid and immovable. It needs a kind of miracle to make it liquefy and flow—the miracle of interpretation and inspiration—wrought most often by the living voice of a wise master, and communicating to the young heart the wonderful secret that some books are alive. Never shall I forget the miracle wrought for me by the reading of Milton's *Comus* by my father in his book-lined study on Brooklyn Heights, and of Cicero's *Letters* by Professor Packard in the Latin class at old Princeton.

The Greeks learned the alphabet from the Phœnicians. But the Phœnicians used it for contracts, deeds, bills of lading, and accounts; the Greeks for poetry and philosophy. Contracts and accounts, of all kinds, are for filing. Literature is of one kind only, the interpretation of life and nature through the imagination in clear and personal words of power and charm. And this is for reading.

To get the good of the library in the school of life you must bring into it something better than a mere bookish taste. You must bring the power to read, between the lines, behind the words, beyond the horizon of the printed page. Philip's question to the chamberlain of Ethiopia was crucial: "Understandest thou what thou readest?"

I want books not to pass the time,

but to fill it with beautiful thoughts and images, to enlarge my world, to give me new friends in the spirit, to purify my ideals and make them clear, to show me the local colour of unknown regions and the bright stars of universal truth.

Time is wasted if we read too much looking-glass fiction, books about our own class and place and period, stories of American college life, society novels, tales in which our own conversation is repeated and our own prejudices are embodied—Kodak prints, Gramophone cylinders! I prefer the real voice, the visible face, things which I can see and hear for myself without waiting for Miss Arabella Tompkins' report of them. When I read, I wish to go abroad, to hear new messages, to meet new people, to get a fresh point of view, to revisit other ages, to listen to the oracles of Delphi and drink deep of the springs of Pieria. The only writer who can tell me anything of real value about my familiar environment is the genius who shows me that after all it is not familiar, but strange, wonderful, crowded with secrets unguessed and possibilities unrealized.

The two things best worth reading about in poetry and fiction are the symbols of nature and the passions of the human heart. I want also an essayist who will clarify life by gentle illumination and lambent humour; a philosopher who will help me to see the reason of things apparently unreasonable; a historian who will show me how peoples have risen and fallen; and a biographer who will let me touch the hand of the great and the good. This is the magic of literature. This is how real books help to educate us in the school of life.

There is no less virtue, but rather more, in events, tasks, duties, obligations, than there is in books. Work itself has a singular power to unfold and develop our nature. The difference is not between working people and thinking people, but between people who work without thinking and people who think while they work.

What is it that you have to do? To weave cloth, to grow fruit, to sell bread, to make a fire, to prepare food, to nurse the sick, to keep house? It matters not. Your task brings you the first lesson of reason—that you must deal with things as they are, not as you imagine or desire them to be. Wet wood will not burn. Fruit trees must have sunshine. Heavy bread will not sell. Sick people have whims. Empty cupboards yield no dinners. The house will not keep itself. Platitudes, no doubt;

but worth more for education than many a metaphysical theory or romantic dream. For when we face these things and realize their meaning, they lead us out of the folly of trying to live in such a world as we would like it to be, and make us live in the world which is.

The mystic visions of the dreamy Orient are a splendid pageant. But for guidance I follow a teacher like Socrates, whose gods were too noble to deceive or masquerade, whose world was a substantial embodiment of divine ideas, and whose men and women were not playthings of Fate or Chance, but living souls, working, struggling, fighting their way to victory.

I do not wish to stay with the nurse and hear fairy tales. I prefer to enter the school of life. In the presence of the mysteries of pain and suffering, under the pressure of disaster or disease, I turn not for counsel to some Scythian soothsayer with her dark incantations and her vague assurances that the evil will vanish if I only close my eyes, but to such a calm, wise teacher as Hippocrates, who says: "As for me, I think that these maladies are divine, like all others, but that none is more divine or more human than another. Each has its natural principle, and none exists without its natural cause."

This is intellectual fortitude. And fortitude is the sentinel and guardian virtue; without it all other virtues are in peril. Daring is inborn, and often born blind. But fortitude is implanted, nurtured, unfolded in the school of life.

I praise the marvellous courage of the human heart, enduring evils, facing perplexities, overcoming obstacles, rising after a hundred falls, building up what gravity pulls down, toiling at

[268]

tasks never finished, relighting extinguished fires, and hoping all things. I like not the implication of Byron's line—"*fair* women and *brave* men"— for women are not less brave than men, but often more brave, though in a different way. Life itself takes them in hand, these delicate and gracious creatures; and if they are worthy and willing, true scholars of experience, educates them in a heroism of the heart which suffers all the more splendidly because it is sensitive, and conquers fear all the more gloriously because it is timorous.

The obstinacy of the materials with which we have to deal, in all kinds of human work, has an educational value. Someone has called it "the total depravity of inanimate things." The phrase would be fit if depravity could be conceived of as beneficent.

No doubt a world in which matter never got out of place and became dirt, in which iron had no flaws and wood no cracks, in which gardens had no weeds and food grew ready cooked, in which clothes never wore out and washing was as easy as the soap-makers' advertisements describe it, in which rules had no exceptions, and things never went wrong, would be a much easier place to live in. But for purposes of training and development it would be worth nothing at all.

It is the resistance that puts us on our mettle: it is the conquest of the reluctant stuff that educates the worker. I wish you enough difficulties to keep you well and make you strong and skilful!

No one can get the full benefit of the school of life who does not welcome the silent and deep instruction of nature. This earth on which we live, these heavens above us, these dumb companions of our work and play, this wondrous living furniture and blossoming drapery of our school-room—all have their lessons to impart. But they will not teach swiftly and suddenly; they will not let us master their meaning in a single course, or sum it all up in a single treatise. Slowly, gradually, with infinite reserves, with delicate confidences, as if they would prolong their instruction that we may not forsake their companionship, they yield up their significance to the student who loves them.

The scientific study of nature is often commended on merely practical grounds. I would honour and praise it for higher reasons—for its power to train the senses in the habit of veracious observation; for its corrective influence upon the audacity of a logic which would attempt to evolve the camel from

the inner consciousness of a philosopher; for its steadying, quieting effect
upon the mind. Poets have indulged
too often in supercilious sneers at the
man of science, the natural philosopher—

> "a fingering slave,
> One that would peep and botanize
> Upon his mother's grave."

The contempt is ill founded; the sneer
is indiscriminate. It is as if one should
speak of the poet as—

> A man of trifling breath,
> One that would flute and sonneteer
> About his sweetheart's death.

Is there any more danger of narrowing the mind by the patient scrutiny of
plants and birds than by the investiga-
tion of ancient documents and annals,
or the study of tropes, metaphors, and
metres? Is it only among men of science
that we find pettiness, and irascibility,

[272]

and domineering omniscience, or do they sometimes occur among historians and poets? It seems to me that there are no more serene and admirable intelligences than those which are often found among the true naturalists. How fine and enviable is their life-long pursuit of their chosen subject. What mind could be happier in its kingdom than that of an Agassiz or a Guyot? What life more beautiful and satisfying than that of a Linnæus or an Audubon?

But for most of us these advanced courses in natural science are impossible. What we must content ourselves with is not really worthy to be called nature-study; it is simply nature-kindergarten. We learn a little about the movements of the stars and clouds; a few names of trees and flowers and birds; some of the many secrets of their life and growth; just the words of one syllable, that is all. And then if we are wise and teachable, we walk with Nature, and let her breathe into our hearts those lessons of humility, and patience, and confidence, and good cheer, and tranquil resignation, and temperate joy, which are her "moral lore"—lessons which lead her scholars onward through a merry youth, and a strong maturity, and a serene old age, and prepare them by the pure companionship of this world for the enjoyment of a better.

The social environment, the human contact in all its forms, plays a large part in the school of life. "The city instructs men," said Simonides.

Conversation is an exchange of ideas: this is what distinguishes it from gossip and chatter. The organization of work, the division of labour, implies and should secure a mutual education of the workers. Some day, when this is better understood, the capitalist will be enlightened and the labour-union civilized.

Even the vexed problem of domestic service is capable of yielding educational results to those who are busy with it. The mistress may learn something of the nature of fair dealing, the responsibilities of command, the essential difference between a carpet-sweeping machine and the girl who pushes it. The servant may learn something of the dignity of doing any kind of work well, the virtue of self-respecting obedience, and the sweet reasonableness of performing the task that is paid for.

I do not think much of the analogy between human society and the bee-hive or the ant-hill, which certain writers are now elaborating in subtle symbolist fashion. It passes over and ignores the vital problem which is ever pressing upon us humans—the problem of reconciling personal claims with the claims of the race. Among the bees and the ants, so far as we can see, the community is all, the individual is nothing. There are no personal aspirations to suppress; no conscious conflicts of duty and desire; no dreams of a better kind of hive, a new and perfected formicary. It is only to repeat themselves, to keep the machine going, to reproduce the same hive, the same ant-hill, that these perfect communisms blindly strive. But human society is less perfect, and therefore more promising. The highest achievements of humanity come from something which, so far as we know, bees and ants do not possess: the sense of imperfection, the desire of advance.

Ideals must be personal before they can become communal. It was not until

the rights of the individual were per-
ceived and recognized, including the
right to the pursuit of happiness, that
the vision of a free and noble state,
capable of progress, dawned upon mankind.

Life teaches all but the obstinate and
mean how to find a place in such a state
and grow therein. A true love of others
is the counterpart of a right love of
self; that is, a love for the better part,
the finer, nobler self, the man that is

"to arise in me,
That the man that I am may cease to be."

Individualism is a fatal poison. But
individuality is the salt of common life.
You may have to live in a crowd, but
you do not have to live like it, nor sub-
sist on its food. You may have your
own orchard. You may drink at a hidden spring. Be yourself if you would
serve others.

[277]

Learn also how to appraise criticism, to value enmity, to get the good of being blamed and evil spoken of. A soft social life is not likely to be very noble. You can hardly tell whether your faiths and feelings are real until they are attacked.

But take care that you defend them with an open mind and by right reason. You are entitled to a point of view, but not to announce it as the centre of the universe. Prejudice, more than anything else, robs life of its educational value. I knew a man who maintained that the chief obstacle to the triumph of Christianity was the practice of infant baptism. I heard a woman say that no one who ate with his knife could be a gentleman. Hopeless scholars these!

What we call society is very narrow. But life is very broad. It includes "the whole world of God's cheerful, fallible men and women." It is not only the famous people and the well-dressed people who are worth meeting. It is everyone who has something to communicate. The scholar has something to say to me, if he be still alive. But I would hear also the traveller, the manufacturer, the soldier, the good workman, the forester, the village school-teacher, the nurse, the quiet observer, the unspoiled child, the skilful housewife. I knew an old German woman, living in a city tenement, who said: "My heart is a little garden, and God is planting flowers there."

"Il faut cultiver son jardin"—yes, but not only that. One should learn also to enjoy the neighbour's garden, however small; the roses straggling over the fence, the scent of lilacs drifting across the road.

There is a great complaint nowadays about the complication of life, especially in its social and material aspects. It is bewildering, confusing, over-straining. It destroys the temper of tranquillity necessary to education. The simple life is recommended, and right-ly, as a refuge from this trouble.

But perhaps we need to understand a little more clearly what simplicity is. It does not consist merely in low ceilings, loose garments, and the absence of *bric-à-brac*. Life may be conventional and artificial in a log cabin. Philistines have their prejudices, and the etiquette of the cotton-mill is often as absurd and burdensome as that of the manor-house.

A little country town, with its inflexible social traditions, its petty animosities and jealousies, its obstinate mistrust of all that is strange, and its crude gossip about all that it cannot comprehend, with its sensitive self-complacency, and its subtle convolutions of parish politics, and its rivalries on a half-inch scale, may be as complicated and as hard to live in as great Babylon itself.

Simplicity, in truth, depends but little on external things. It can live in broadcloth or homespun; it can eat white bread or black. It is not outward, but inward. A certain openness of mind to learn the daily lessons of the school of life; a certain willingness of heart to give and to receive that extra service, that gift beyond the strict measure of debt, which makes friendship possible; a certain clearness of spirit to perceive the best in things and people, to love it without fear and to cleave to it without mistrust; a peaceable sureness of affection and taste; a gentle straightforwardness of action; a kind sincerity of speech—these are the marks of the simple life. It cometh not with observation, for it is within you. I have seen it in a hut. I have seen it in a palace. And wherever it is found it is the best prize of the school of life, the badge of a scholar well-beloved of the Master.

FINIS